ALSO BY TOM FITTON

The Corruption Chronicles

Clean House

A Republic Under Assault

RIGHTS AND FREEDOMS IN PERIL

AN INVESTIGATIVE REPORT ON THE LEFT'S ATTACK ON AMERICA

TOM FITTON

Threshold Editions

New York   London   Toronto   Sydney   New Delhi

Threshold Editions
An Imprint of Simon & Schuster, LLC
1230 Avenue of the Americas
New York, NY 10020

First Threshold Editions hardcover edition October 2024

THRESHOLD EDITIONS and colophon are trademarks of Simon & Schuster, LLC

For information about special discounts for bulk purchases, please contact Simon & Schuster Special Sales at 1-866-506-1949 or business@simonandschuster.com.

The Simon & Schuster Speakers Bureau can bring authors to your live event. For more information or to book an event, contact the Simon & Schuster Speakers Bureau at 1-866-248-3049 or visit our website at www.simonspeakers.com.

Interior design by Jaime Putorti

Manufactured in the United States of America

10 9 8 7 6 5 4 3 2 1

Library of Congress Cataloging-in-Publication Data is available.

ISBN 978-1-6680-6214-2
ISBN 978-1-6680-6216-6 (ebook)

To the millions of Judicial Watch supporters and other American patriots concerned about the preservation of our battered but still-standing constitutional republic for their children and grandchildren

CONTENTS

RIGHTS AND FREEDOMS IN PERIL

INTRODUCTION

We are at a decisive moment in the history of the republic. The Biden regime and allied leftists have taken unprecedented steps to undermine our Constitution and our system of government.

The Biden White House is advancing the Left's agenda at full pace with little regard for the US Constitution and the rule of law. Biden's agencies and Democratic politicians in several states have turned the law itself into a cudgel against their political opponents. They have violated our rights and freedoms while covering up their own corruption. These abuses need to be stopped.

The Biden administration smirks as members of their party work overtime to imprison Donald Trump, their greatest political enemy and rival. Yet as liberals in public office and the media celebrate trumped-up charges, the most fervent advocates of prosecuting Trump cannot state in clear terms the crimes for which he was unfairly convicted.

"Paying hush money!" we are told. Well, that's not illegal and not even unethical. Case closed. End of inquiry. Yet Trump was prosecuted for non-crimes by a Democratic Party politician. The political prosecution was enabled by a judge who is a conflicted political donor to Joe Biden, whose bias against Trump during the process will go down in judicial infamy.

My official Judicial Watch reaction to the sham verdict was blunt and will hopefully be vindicated by responsible courts in the end:

> Pure corruption. Judicial Watch denounces this absurd verdict and Soviet-style criminal proceeding that has so abused President Trump. What just happened to Trump up in New York is criminal.
>
> The guilty verdict against Trump is no surprise considering the rigged, kangaroo court proceedings run by a biased, conflicted judge and an unethical, politicized Democratic Party prosecution team. Today is a terrible day for the rule of law that will go down in infamy. This whole process is compromised, and this verdict should be overturned in an emergency fashion.
>
> The evidence shows that Trump committed no crimes, and this is a prosecution about "nothing." This and other Democratic Party political prosecutions of Trump are an abomination under law and are destabilizing to our nation.

The cases against Trump, in his New York civil and criminal trials as well as his Georgia criminal indictment and two federal indictments, are entirely political. This was demonstrated clearly when reports emerged of President Biden's "frustration" with his attorney general's delay in getting Trump indicted. Attorney General Merrick Garland, the reports suggested, was not moving fast enough; President Biden wanted the investigations into his political opponent to move faster. This animus coming from the very top was shown again when reports claimed that a top Biden appointee at the Justice Department magically got hired up in New York to manage the cases against Trump there.

Everything they say about Trump is a projection of their own actions. They accused him of rigging the 2016 election in collusion with Russia, when it turned out that the Obama White House and the

Hillary Clinton campaign created that story using federal law enforcement resources, a story they knew to be false.

They said he would throttle the First Amendment while the federal government under Biden and well-funded left-wing private partners have proudly and publicly threatened and pushed for the censorship of tens of millions of Americans.

They accused Trump of massive corruption and shady business involvement with disreputable regimes. But the Clinton Foundation and the Biden family business were neck deep in deals with China, Ukraine, and dodgy Central Asian republics. They critiqued Trump's standard real estate business, when the Biden family had countless shell companies and bank accounts for distributing the proceeds of obviously shady payments from abroad.

....

They said Trump would bring fascism to America and lock up all his opponents, but they're currently trying a former president in unprecedented cases that can only be described as partisan witch hunts. If Donald Trump had authoritarian ambitions, he did a pretty bad job of bringing them to fruition. The Biden administration meanwhile has sworn revenge on Trump and is actively punishing anyone associated with him.

As of this writing, the regime is engaged in a lawfare campaign to imprison Trump for life and to liquidate all his assets. They are subverting the core principles of our democracy as they gaslight the population with outlandish claims that Trump, and each and every one of his supporters, poses a threat to our "democracy."

I make these points not as part of a campaign screed but as a sober analysis of the state of our nation. Will we allow the civil rights of those on the wrong side of the Big Government socialist Leviathan to be trampled? Our elections to be rigged by abusive prosecutors seeking to jail candidates and their supporters? The fabric of our nation to be torn about woke racism? Our very country to end under the deluge of purposeful and never-ending illegal alien invasion the likes of which have never been before seen in the history of Western civilization?

A strong constitutional republic demands an informed citizenry. Judicial Watch was founded to inform the public as to what their government is doing in their name. America is, technically speaking, the freest country in the world when it comes to exposing government operations. Talk to a European and ask them how they go about getting the emails and other records and communications that comprise the workings of the state. They will likely laugh at your naivety.

My colleagues at Judicial Watch made it our life's work to figure out where the secrets are, and to ferret them out painstakingly with requests for information, and lawsuits where necessary. We seek to expose lies to sunlight and to disinfect the innards of a system under stress from the rising extremists who seek to end the American way.

The last four years of rule by the Biden administration—which some think of as the third Obama administration—have been the most corrupt in modern memory. (Though I often sarcastically remark that "Joe Biden is the most corrupt president since he was vice president"!)

The challenge to our republic comes from Biden and other left partisans who have embraced a totalitarian, communist approach to political battles. Destroy and undermine constitutional institutions, censor and jail your political enemies, and exercise power and ignore law in a way that is unmoored from *any* constitutional or legal restraint.

....

The lies aren't harmless. They have real-world consequences and are currently tearing at the fabric of our republic. Corruption is undermining our government's capacity to make good on its promise to protect the rights of citizens. Instead, at the highest levels, bureaucrats and politicians are undermining those rights to advance a political agenda.

Covid was a pandemic, but the real contagion threating our republic is corruption and contempt for the rights of man.

The 2020 election was declared the most secure and honest election in American history. Some dared asked how that could have been the case, when it was conducted in such an unprecedented and untrustworthy manner.

Claiming that there were irregularities in the 2020 election became grounds for suspicion and criminal investigation. Raising a question about Biden's victory could literally mean the feds coming to knock on your door. Well-known political and media figures were kicked off social media after January 6, including President Trump himself. The "insurrection" of that day was composed of a rally that turned into a riot at the Capitol in Washington. But the Capitol melee was quickly cast as the worst political violence in American history, the worst day since the Civil War, a moment when American democracy was almost lost, and a day of unimaginable bloodshed.

Only one person was an actual homicide victim on January 6, and her name was Ashli Babbitt. Shot dead by a trigger-happy police officer who was protected, rewarded, and promoted.

The Biden administration and their allies in the mainstream media have tried to make everyone observe January 6 as a new day of infamy, but it just didn't take.

The Biden years will be remembered for the dissolution of the American border. Under his watch, between 8 and 10 million migrants crossed over that we know about. Customs and Border Protection ceased to be a force that guarded the frontier and became a welcome wagon for our newest Americans. Venezuela emptied its prisons and asylums and pointed the former occupants north. All were welcomed, given cell phones and bus tickets, and told to make themselves available for asylum hearings that were scheduled for 2035.

And these millions are looked upon with excitement by leftists who see masses of new voters and power centers for their anti-American projects.

Politicized indictments, ruined elections, invasions, and compromised politicians have placed our republican form of government in peril.

There is a way forward, but we must be diligent about understanding the scope and detail of the peril. There is a way forward for America, but first we must learn the truths and secrets described in this book.

CHAPTER 1

PLANNED CHAOS AT THE BORDER

On his first day in office, Joe Biden set about undoing as much of his predecessor's agenda and accomplishments as possible. Of the seventeen executive orders he issued on January 20, 2021, more than one-third of them related to immigration and the presence of millions of noncitizens in the country.[1]

The "Day One" orders promulgated by the new Biden administration guaranteed that illegal immigrants would be counted for the purposes of congressional apportionment. This would ensure that non-voting residents of congressional districts would plump up the population numbers, creating what used to be called "rotten boroughs," or districts where actual citizens are underrepresented.

The orders also ended the so-called Muslim ban, which restricted entry from a select number of countries that are closely tied to international terror networks. The restrictions, which always contained exemptions for worthy cases, were widely denounced by the media, academia, and left-wing advocates as racist and Islamophobic when they were first imposed in 2017. Biden's reversal of Trump's policy went beyond simply lifting the restrictions. It sought to rectify the supposed injustice of the past and "restart visa processing for affected countries and to swiftly develop a proposal to restore fairness and remedy the harms caused by the bans, especially for individuals stuck in the waiver process and those who had immigrant visas denied."

President Biden ordered the US government, in other words, to seek out foreigners who had been denied entry and repair the damage by offering them admission. This principle aligns and describes the outlook of the Left regarding immigration: Everyone has an affirmative right to live in the United States. Any restriction on immigration is presumptively racist. Not letting someone move here is a violation of their rights as a potential American, even if they have never stepped foot in the United States.

"This is an important step," Biden's order read, "in providing relief to individuals and families harmed by this Trump Administration policy that is inconsistent with American values."

Biden issued other orders, too. One order was to "Stop Border Wall Construction" as "wasteful" and possibly illegal, and replace the focus on building a wall with "smart border controls," focused on high-tech scanners to detect the presence of contraband. Another order protected 700,000 people who had been brought to the United States illegally as minors, and yet another extended "deferred enforced departure" protection to Liberians residing in America.

Another revoked a Trump policy "that directed harsh and extreme immigration enforcement," specifically the arrest and deportation of illegal immigrants. "The task of enforcing the immigration laws is complex and requires setting priorities to best serve the national interest," Biden's executive order explained. And the "complexity" of the laws demanded that, in effect, we stop enforcing them.

During his 2020 campaign, Biden indicated he would stop deporting illegal immigrants. At a February CNN "town hall," the former vice president spoke in favor of a secure border, but cautioned, "We have a right to protect the border. But the idea—and by the way, nobody—and some of you are going to get mad at me with this—

but nobody is going to be deported in my first 100 days until we get through the point that we find out the only rationale for deportation will be whether or not—whether or not you've committed a felony while in the country."[2]

Advocates pushed the Biden campaign to formalize this pledge into a campaign promise. Initially resistant, the campaign folded to pressure from the Latino Victory Fund. "Vice President Biden is absolutely committed to a 100-day moratorium on any deportations of people already in the United States," the Biden campaign announced, promising to "center all the issues important to Latinos at the heart of this movement as we work to send Donald Trump and his unmitigated assault on our national values packing."[3]

All of this meant that the first week of the Biden administration set the stage for what has emerged as possibly the most destructive policy in the nation's history. Under Joe Biden, America has essentially opened its borders and given up any pretense of caring who comes in and why they are here. It is estimated that between 8 and 10 million migrants have entered the country. This mad rush from around the world has increased the American population by as much as 3 percent, stressed local budgets, depressed wages, raised housing costs, and threatens to destabilize society.

American law allows people with a genuine and credible fear of persecution—based on race, religion, nationality, membership in a particular social group, or political opinion—to receive protection from the American government. A person fleeing from a despotic regime may claim asylum, and is entitled to a hearing to determine whether the claim is valid.

Providing asylum is a humanitarian policy that most governments offer to one extent or another. But advocates for open borders have advertised asylum as a loophole to allow illegal aliens to remain in the country under legal cover. You don't have to prove that you were persecuted in your country of origin to receive a conditional permit of entry; that comes later, when you go to court. But the flood of asylees is so massive that court dates are set for years in the future.

Most of these cases have no legitimacy and will fail in court. The vast majority of migrants to the US are here for the proverbial "better life." They want to work, make money, and take advantage of the opportunities America has to offer.

But migration for economic reasons is not grounds for asylum. America already has Americans who need work and taxpayers who need relief. American immigration policy must be set according to the needs and wants of American citizens as expressed through the democratic process, which has already established a set of laws that govern the rules of admission. When an American president decides to ignore the law and effectively stop defending the border, he is violating his oath of office. And by effectively overturning the laws of our republic, he is as much an "insurrectionist" as any Proud Boy rushing the US Capitol.

Judicial Watch is in the forefront of fighting to protect the American people and the sanctity of their citizenship. The leftist regime dreams of one world ruled by a slate of unelected experts in government agencies, global oversight bodies, and non-governmental organizations, abetted by their allies in universities, pliant mega-corporations, and the mass media. The American idea of rule by the people, in whom sovereignty is vested by God, is anathema to the globalist vision. Open borders and the devaluation of citizenship are key to this program. This attack on citizens and our republican form of government through a mass invasion of foreign nationals, as much as anything, motivates Judicial Watch and our fight for the rule of law.

....

When President Trump stepped up enforcement at the southern border, Immigration and Customs Enforcement (ICE) continued the usual policy of arresting people and processing them for deportation. Many migrants crossing with children—theirs or someone else's—would be caught and placed in separate facilities from those children. This is typically how arrests work, even for regular crimes committed domestically by citizens. If you or I were pulled over for impaired driving with children in the car, we would be taken into custody, and the police would have to figure out what to do with the kids. If there were no adults with a legal claim to guardianship, the children would become wards of the state until some other arrangement could be found.

The Obama administration was the first to start separating adults from children at the border for processing, and it was under Obama that the first "kids in cages" pictures became public. When Trump came to office, he continued the policy but expanded it by taking a zero tolerance approach, as a means of discouraging the common practice of using children as a kind of ticket for entry into America.

The Obama-Trump policy of suppressing international child trafficking, one might presume, would be a point that both parties could rally around.

But the Left and its allies in the media seized on Trump's border security measures related to children and exploited the associated imagery to present the Trump administration as fascistic, and ICE as a modern-day version of the Gestapo. Democrat politicians rushed to the border to pose for pictures weeping over the plight of children ripped from their mothers' arms.

A photo of a two-year-old girl crying while her mother was patted down went viral and won the 2019 World Press Photo award. The picture was widely cited as evidence of the inhumanity of Trump's family separation policy, though the photographer did explain that the baby was only crying because her mother had put her down for a moment, not because of anything catastrophic. It turned out that the child was not separated from her mother even after their detention, because the policy did not apply to such small children.

In any event, Trump rescinded his zero-tolerance policy after six weeks, and as a result, according to the *Washington Post*, "The controversy and attention the episode generated—and Trump's declaration that children would no longer be separated—was something smugglers quickly seized on. They began telling would-be clients that children were a passport into the United States."[4]

The Left is playing a neat game. They deny that strict enforcement discourages illegal immigration. They scream about human rights when the government tries to enforce the law. And then when immigration shoots up after enforcement decreases, they shrug their shoulders and blame America for having created such terrible conditions abroad, and American workers for being too lazy. No matter how one slices it, open-border policies and their defenders are anti-American.

....

One major problem that predates the Biden or even Obama administrations is the weaponization of the principle of federalism to protect illegal aliens, even criminals, from deportation. "Sanctuary" jurisdictions refuse to cooperate with federal immigration authorities in arresting or detaining illegals, and even forbid the local police from sharing information with their federal partners.

Cities such as New York, Chicago, Philadelphia, San Francisco, and Los Angeles proudly boast about being "sanctuaries" for illegal aliens. The principle of sanctuary in regard to immigration dates to the eighties, and was originally supposed to encourage illegal immigrants to report crimes, go to the hospital, or enroll their children in school without fear of being reported to the authorities. But as time went on, radical advocates transformed the passive definition of sanctuary to be much more active, to the point where cities effectively are turning themselves into robbers' caves.

In March 2021, Judicial Watch was able to announce that its taxpayer lawsuit against the San Francisco Sheriff Department's sanctuary policy uncovered that more than 2,400 criminal illegal aliens were released under the department's policy on communications with Immigration and Customs Enforcement about criminal illegal aliens in the sheriff's custody.

Judicial Watch noted in a court filing that the sheriff's office's policy, "is so effective in regulating immigration and obstructing Congress' purposes under federal immigration law that, in over 2,401 known instances, it has never resulted in ICE taking into custody a single alien, not even aliens with significant criminal backgrounds wanted for removal."[5]

Our 2016 lawsuit argued that the sheriff department's restrictions on communications with ICE conflict with federal immigration law and attempt to regulate immigration and are therefore invalid.

Judicial Watch's court filing included expert testimony detailing specific examples of egregious criminal behavior of illegal aliens that the sheriff's office had in custody who were released without consultation with ICE:

- A citizen of Cuba faced charges for burglary and a parole violation, with a prior burglary conviction.
- A citizen of Vietnam faced charges for robbery, battery, and assault.
- A citizen of Ethiopia was charged with assault with a deadly weapon, assault on a peace officer, receiving stolen property, a parole violation, and had prior convictions for stolen property crimes.
- A citizen of Mexico had a long list of current and prior offenses, including convictions for assault with a deadly weapon, robbery, felony assault, false imprisonment, burglary, vehicle theft, and

probation violations, including one revocation of probation. This individual appeared to have been arrested at least nine times between January 2015 and March 2020.

- A citizen of Honduras was facing instant charges of burglary. His five-page rap sheet included prior convictions on felonies such as burglary while in possession of a concealed, loaded firearm, giving false information to an officer, child endangerment, theft, domestic violence, robbery, assault, and violating a restraining order.
- Another citizen of Mexico was facing instant charges of robbery, domestic violence, and assault, and was also the subject of an ICE detainer and warrant of arrest after a biometric match with DHS records. The alien had three recent, separate, prior felony convictions: two for auto theft and one for burglary, which had occurred over a fifteen-month period ending two and one-half years prior to the instant offense.
- A citizen of Ukraine was arrested and held to answer for a felony burglary charge, along with false imprisonment, receiving stolen property, threatening an officer, and a firearms charge. Two years prior, he was convicted on a robbery charge, among other offense.
- Another citizen of Mexico was held to answer on felony burglary charges, false imprisonment, and adult kidnapping charges. The alien had prior burglary convictions, one occurring one year prior to the instant charge, and another occurring four years prior, for which he was sentenced to 364 days plus probation.
- A citizen of Cambodia was facing instant charges for assault with a deadly weapon, murder, and a loaded firearm violation.

"Judicial Watch's taxpayer lawsuit shows that the San Francisco Sheriff's sanctuary policy is not only unlawful but is a clear and present danger to the public safety," I said at the time. But I had no idea how insane things would become.

....

It is impossible to overstate the impact of the wave of migration that has flooded our borders in the last few years, especially on American communities on or near the border. Millions of unvetted people, many speaking little or no English, possessing only what they carry, have shown up in small cities or towns and essentially thrown themselves on the charity and goodwill of the locals. Moreover, the federal government has enabled and facilitated the transportation of these illegal aliens throughout the country in the dead of night.

Local law enforcement agencies nationwide have been overwhelmed with criminal activity linked to the huge increase in illegal immigration, and families are being exposed to violence associated with drug trafficking and transnational gangs. As early as May 2021, just a few months into the Biden presidency, hundreds of sheriffs across the United States slammed the administration's "reckless and irresponsible" open-border policies, exposing innocent citizens to illegal alien violence, in a letter titled "Help America's Sheriffs Keep Our Neighborhoods and Communities Safe by Halting Illegal Immigration." The document asserts that the crisis began when Biden was vice president.

"In a myriad of ways, you and your administration are encouraging and sanctioning lawlessness and the victimization of the people of the United States of America, all in the name of mass illegal immigration," the sheriffs wrote. "What is most troubling to America's Sheriffs is that you and your administration were well aware that this crisis would happen when you ceased construction of the border wall and changed border security policies."[6]

The sheriff who wrote the letter, Thomas M. Hodgson in Bristol County, Massachusetts, sent it to his counterparts throughout the US, and 275 sheriffs in 39 states quickly signed it. Hodgson authored it after government figures revealed a record number of illegal immigrant minors entered the country from Mexico. Around the same time, the

US Border Patrol disclosed that it arrested more than twice as many criminal migrants in the first six months of fiscal year 2021 than it did in all of 2020. In the first half of this fiscal year, the Border Patrol apprehended 5,018 "criminal aliens" compared to 2,438 in all of fiscal year 2020. The agency defines criminal aliens as individuals who have been convicted of one or more crimes, whether in the US or abroad, prior to interdiction by federal agents.

It is important to note that the data, which covered fiscal years 2016 through 2021, showed a steady decline in criminal alien arrests during the Trump administration after a peak of 12,842 arrests in 2016 under Obama. By 2017 it dipped to 8,531, then 6,698 in 2018 and 4,260 in 2019, before the low of 2,438 in 2020. The criminal aliens busted by the Border Patrol in the first few months of 2021 include 982 convicted of possessing illegal drugs or trafficking; 576 convicted of assault, battery, and domestic violence; 832 guilty of driving under the influence; 381 convicted of burglary, robbery, larceny, theft, and fraud; 265 sex offenders; and 162 guilty of illegal weapons possession, transport, and trafficking.

The stats also reveal that 2,765 of the criminal aliens arrested in the first half of 2021 were previously deported after illegal entry or illegal reentry. Additionally, seizures of methamphetamine along the Mexican border increased an astounding 91 percent between February and March 2021, according to Customs and Border Patrol (CBP) figures. Heroin seizures went up 22 percent during the same period.[7]

The situation along the Mexican border quickly reached a boiling point, with a record number of illegal immigrants arriving in just a few months thanks to Biden administration policies. Veteran frontline federal agents told Judicial Watch they had never seen anything like it. Even sleepy little towns unaccustomed to the devastating impact large influxes have on bigger cities near major crossings were impacted by the storm of migrants. For instance, Judicial Watch interviewed veteran ranchers and business owners in the usually tranquil Arizona town of Sonoita, population of about 800, in the aftermath of a series of crimes committed by illegal aliens and human smugglers (coyotes) that left residents shocked. In just a few days there were two home invasion robberies, and two local stores were burglarized by a group of illegal immigrants who had just been released into their community by the US Border Patrol in the predawn hours. The problem is only getting worse, locals say, because federal agents are overwhelmed with the onslaught of migrants, and more are being released into communities near the border.

Many Americans dream of being able to start over, to free themselves of debts or personal histories. This is impossible for average citizens in today's United States, where our permanent digital record follows us everywhere. But if you are a criminal from anywhere else in the world, or if you are just tired of supporting your family, or you have a lot of debts you would prefer not to pay, you can simply show up at the American border without any documentation and declare yourself to be whoever you want. America is now like the French Foreign Legion, where you can get a brand-new identity. Of course, in the Foreign Legion you have to serve as a soldier, whereas in open-borders America you don't have to do anything to get your new life.

....

In April 2021, Judicial Watch filed a Freedom of Information Act lawsuit against the US Department of Health and Human Services (HHS) for records about assaults on and abuse of unaccompanied alien children (UAC) in HHS custody. The lawsuit was filed against Health and Human Services after the HHS denied a February 26, 2021, FOIA request for:

> All summaries from individual case files of reports of physical
> and/or sexual abuse or assault of Unaccompanied Alien
> Children under the care of HHS, its sub-agencies, and/or

volunteer agencies, contractors, grantees, and sub-grantees, to include all segregable, non-exempt information.

Records reflecting aggregated data of physical and/or sexual abuse and assault of UACs under the care of HHS, its sub-agencies, and or volunteer agencies, contractors, grantees, and sub-grantees.

Our interest was piqued when Texas welfare officials received three reports of abuse and neglect at the Freeman Coliseum in San Antonio, where more than 1,300 migrant children reportedly had been held. The site is one of several set up to handle the recent surge.

This report came on the heels of claims that multiple facilities where children are being held are unsafe.

"We are concerned that the surge of migrants seeking to take advantage of the Biden administration's lax immigration policies has resulted in the foreseeable abuse of children, as overwhelmed federal authorities are ill-equipped to handle the huge number of children crossing the border. The unprecedented secrecy and censorship surrounding these sites compounds the problem and limits accountability," I said at the time. "Our lawsuit aims to expose the full truth about this particularly troubling consequence of the Biden administration's lawlessness on immigration."[8]

Sure enough, Judicial Watch uncovered HHS records in July 2018 revealing that in multiple cases, UACs processed during the Obama administration were assaulted by government employees.

Judicial Watch began investigating this matter in 2014 when a wave of UACs swamped the southwest border. Since that time, Judicial Watch has been investigating incidents of violence, drug trafficking, human trafficking, and other criminal activities, as well as whether migrant children were being abused while in US shelters.

Incidentally, it is amazing to see how the Left has selective concern about the fate and condition of kids who are detained while crossing the border. Congresswoman Alexandria Ocasio-Cortez was famously photographed collapsing in a state of utter grief during a visit to a border detention center in 2018—though it was demonstrated that she was basically looking at a parking lot—but she has been noticeably silent about the issue since Trump left office.

As a result of our FOIA lawsuit, the Office of Refugee Resettlement released information indicating that sexual abuse against minors in detention centers was rampant, across the country. In just five weeks at the beginning of 2021, thirty-three cases of sexual abuse were documented at centers from Florida to Michigan to Texas. In some cases staff were implicated; in others "non-staff adults" were alleged to have committed abuse. Judicial Watch also forced the Department of Health and Human Services to release data on physical abuse involving illegal immigrant minors in custody of the federal government or contracted providers. The documentation, released in August 2021, details a horrific environment of abuse and beating among the residents that reads like something out of *Fight Club*.[9]

The Biden administration quickly implemented its project of transporting illegal aliens throughout the country, often in the dead of night to small, outlying airports where media coverage might be thin. Judicial Watch sued to obtain information on these flights, and garnered some details on some of them, but the extent of the program has been so vast and secret that it is unlikely that it will ever be fully known.

We did manage to get some information, and what we obtained offers a window into the largest human trafficking endeavor in American history. The American government, without the consent of the localities involved, set about perfusing the nation with millions of illegal aliens.

Judicial Watch sued the Administration for Children and Families, a division of HHS, in October 2022, after the agency failed to respond to a May 2021 request for information regarding:

All documents related to the preparation and logistics involved in the transportation of Unaccompanied Alien Children (UACs) to and from Chattanooga's Wilson Air Center on May 14, 2021, and

All ACF officials' internal email communications related to the transportation of UACs to and from Chattanooga's Wilson Air Center on May 14, 2021.

The records include a May 15 email from a person whose name is redacted to an unnamed person at MVM Inc's Office of Refugee Resettlement (ORR) Transport DFW (Dallas Fort Worth) Command Center detailing charter flights.

One flight traveling from SAN-OKC-CHA-EWR [San Diego, Oklahoma City, Chattanooga, Newark airports] via "Swift Air," which was operating a Boeing 737 with "148 seats" (likely the number of passengers). It indicates that there would be two buses at the San Diego Convention Center, two buses in Oklahoma City, two buses in Chattanooga, and two buses at Newark.

A second flight, from MFE-ELP-EWR [McAllen, El Paso, Newark] also via "Swift Air," and a 737, with 150 seats, notes: "Pecos [TX] will be bused to ELP [El Paso] to catch charter flight. 1 bus will report 0800. 2 buses to report at 0800 at Delphi EIS [Delphi Emergency Intake Site]."

The records also include a May 13, 2021, email thread regarding an Administration for Children and Families' (ACF) Office of Refugee Resettlement transport of minors from Kay Baily Hutchison Convention Center in Dallas on Friday, May 14, 2021, before dawn, at three a.m.

RF1 Badging then replies, "Please be advised that the following UCs [Unaccompanied Children] . . . does not match in our system." He then proceeds to list the details of nine children.

Also in this thread is an email from an individual at Culmen International stating that one of the minors is "not cleared to travel."

The records include a list for a charter of thirty-six children from Honduras, Guatemala, Mexico, and El Salvador. A handwritten note on the spreadsheet says: "Dallas to Tennessee Air Charter Flight 5/14/2021." The record notes that the children are to be transported to these shelters: La Casa de Sidney, Lincoln Hall Boys' Haven, Children's Home of Kingston, Children's Village Shelter, and Cayuga Center TFC. It indicates three of the minors are "reunifications." (Chattanooga's unaccompanied migrant minor housing facility, La Casa de Sidney, was closed in 2021 after reports of runaways and sexual battery.)

An undated "Transfer of Custody" form indicates the transfer of six Guatemalan and Honduran children from "KBH" [likely Kay Bailey Hutchison Convention Center in Dallas] to La Casa de Sidney.[10]

Please keep in mind that the above itinerary is just a snapshot of one evening and one transit point—Chattanooga, Tennessee's fourth-largest city. When we consider that this operation has been going on for years, across America, and involves the transportation of adults, the scale of the scandal becomes horrendous to contemplate.

These shocking documents provide a small but important window into how the Biden administration effectively trafficking unaccompanied alien children, dropping them off in city after city like items for delivery. The Biden open-borders crisis is resulting in the most massive child and human trafficking operation in the history of humanity.

....

Republican concern about these flights did little to stop them. The federal government has transported hundreds of thousands of illegal aliens around the country, by plane and bus, spreading them into distant communities. Reports circulate of commercial flights mostly filled with bewildered-looking obvious recent immigrants, shepherded by social service administrators, likely employed by government contractors such as Lutheran Immigration and Refugee Services (now rebranded as "Global Refuge") or the Hebrew Immigrant Aid Society.

Judicial Watch has been keeping an active eye on these faith-based human-trafficking organizations that operate in the name of charity and good works. In February 2022, we filed a Freedom of Information Act lawsuit alongside Catholic Vote Civic Action for records of communication between the US Department of Homeland Security (DHS) and the US Department of Health and Human Services with Catholic organizations near the Texas border that were aiding illegal immigrants.

This lawsuit was filed in Washington, DC, after both the US Customs and Border Patrol and HHS failed to respond to FOIA requests designed to uncover details on the shadow network, funded with tax dollars, that complete the work of the cartels in moving millions of illegal aliens into America. Our first request was for all communications between the US Customs and Border Patrol and any of the following:

- The Diocese of Brownsville (San Juan, Texas);
- Bishop Daniel E. Flores in his capacity as Bishop of the Diocese of Brownsville, Texas;
- Catholic Charities of the Rio Grande Valley (CCRGV);
- Sister Norma Pimentel in her capacity as the Executive Director of CCRGV; or
- The Humanitarian Respite Center in McAllen, Texas.

Our second FOIA request was for all communications between the US Customs and Border Patrol and the US Conference of Catholic Bishops regarding any of the following:

1. Catholic Charities of the Rio Grande Valley (CCRGV);
2. Sister Norma Pimentel in her capacity as the Executive Director of CCRGV; or
3. the Humanitarian Respite Center in McAllen, Texas.

Sister Pimentel, in a February 3 interview, acknowledged her charity is reimbursed with tax dollars to buy "very few" plane and bus tickets for illegal aliens to move throughout the United States.[11]

In July 2021, a Texas police officer encountered a Covid-positive illegal immigrant family at a fast-food restaurant near the border who had been released by Border Patrol. The family told the officer that Catholic Charities of the Rio Grande Valley "had booked all the rooms in the hotel to house undocumented immigrants detained by Border Patrol."

The police added that "Border Patrol was quarantining other undocumented individuals who were Covid positive, or showed symptoms of illness, then handing them over to the nonprofit. Catholic Charities would in turn place the undocumented individuals in hotels . . . "

On July 28, 2021, Texas governor Greg Abbott, taking aim at the "private" enablers of the illegal alien invasion, issued an executive order halting the transportation of illegal immigrants by any person other than "a federal, state or local law-enforcement official."

"Americans have the right to know how the Biden administration is using tax dollars to conspire with 'charities' and release illegal immigrants into their communities," I said at the time.[12]

Even more bizarre than the Biden administration's exercising mass population transfer across the entire nation of immigrants who crossed the border illegally, news emerged that the White House saved 320,000 foreign nationals the hassle of walking here by flying them direct from their home countries. That's right—in order to mitigate the bad optics of 15,000 people swarming across the southern border every day, the Biden team decided to cut out the middleman and just fly "eligible" migrants straight from Cuba, Haiti, Venezuela, and Nicaragua.

These migrants are allowed in under the president's "parole" authority, which, under a 1952 law, allows him to admit people "only on a case-by-case basis for urgent humanitarian reasons or significant public benefit." The Associated Press ran a laughable "debunking" report to clarify that the migrants admitted under this program were not flown in "secretly," and that the admissions were all vetted and approved. The AP did acknowledge that Biden has used "parole" admissions far more than any other president, and has granted at least one million parole-based entry visas.

Nevertheless, as the Center for Immigration Studies discovered, Customs and Border Protection will not release the names of the forty-three American airports that received these foreign shipments of human cargo. But New York, Chicago, and Boston appear to be among the most frequently visited, based on spikes in passenger volume.[13]

....

Given the federal government's abdication of its most basic and sacred responsibility—defense of the national borders—several border states decided to assume the burden of keeping the homeland secure. A Texas border security initiative heavily criticized by Democrats and the media has apprehended hundreds of thousands of illegal immigrants—including thousands of criminals—and seized millions of lethal doses of fentanyl.[14]

Known as Operation Lone Star, the project was launched by Governor Greg Abbott in March 2021 as the illegal immigration crisis gripped his border state. Essentially the Texas Department of Public Safety (DPS) and the Texas National Guard are picking up the slack for the federal government, which in normal times worked to protect the famously porous southern border.

Texas had to take charge to combat the smuggling of people and drugs, the governor's office wrote in the 2021 press release announcing Operation Lone Star, which integrates DPS with the Texas National Guard and deploys air, ground, marine, and tactical border security assets to high-threat areas to prevent Mexican cartels and other criminal elements from smuggling drugs and humans into the state.

"The crisis at our southern border continues to escalate because of Biden administration policies that refuse to secure the border and invite illegal immigration," Abbott said at the time. The governor's office assures that the operation continues to fill the "dangerous gaps left by the Biden administration's refusal to secure the border." Every arrested individual and every ounce of drugs seized by Operation Lone Star would have otherwise made their way into communities across the nation due to the president's open-border policies, Texas officials point out.

Operation Lone Star is succeeding despite detractors on the Left. Since the multi-agency effort was launched, more than 500,000 illegal immigrants have been apprehended and over 40,000 criminals have been arrested. Texas state law enforcement also seized a startling number of drugs, over 469 million lethal doses of fentanyl.

To satisfy the hunger of sanctuary cities to shelter, feed, and clothe illegal alien invaders, Texas has bused more than 100,000 migrants to these redoubts of Christian charity. Since the Democrat-run cities have been the primary proponents of a collapsed border, it makes sense that they should reap their share of the harvest of their policies. Strangely, these blue cities—primarily Chicago, New York City, and Washington, DC—have only responded with outrage, and demanded federal action. Not to close the border, of course—but to pay for the cost of lodging all these "newest Americans."

In Biden's first year as president, federal agents apprehended

1,659,206 illegal immigrants at the southwest border, breaking the previous high of 1,643,679 in 2000. To put things in perspective, during Donald Trump's last year as president federal agents arrested 400,651 illegal aliens along the Mexican border.

But as the Biden presidency progresses, the crisis worsens. Fiscal year 2022 started with a bang, a 137 percent increase in the first quarter over the final quarter of 2021. By the end of 2022, the Border Patrol arrested a record-breaking 2.4 million migrants, up from an already shocking high of 1.7 million in 2021. The numbers only went up in 2023, and 2024 is on pace to see 4 million arrests.[15]

America is on course to add 11 million illegal aliens to the 11 or 12 million that we've been told are here already. But in reality, those are almost certainly lowball numbers, and I've been hearing the open borders crowd talk about "11 million undocumented immigrants" for at least twenty-five years. In 2018, researchers at Yale announced that the number was probably closer to 22 million.[16] The real number is a matter of debate; some put the total closer to 40 or 50 million. I'm not a demographer, but I'm not naïve, either. I'd be surprised if we had fewer than 25 million illegals here before Biden took office. And the number will probably top out around 40 million—assuming the Democrats don't remain in office.

....

Operation Lone Star has seen the arrest of thousands of gang members—mostly from the famously violent Mara Salvatrucha (MS-13)—and dozens of people on the national terrorist watchlist. Federal agents also confiscated thousands of pounds of drugs, mainly methamphetamine. The unprecedented numbers reflect a chaotic Mexican border region rife with lawlessness that has inevitably seeped north into many parts of the United States.

Naturally enough, the Biden Department of Justice couldn't allow a successful state-led border control program to continue. The DoJ wanted to pursue a civil rights case against Texas, based on the idea that it was discriminatory on the basis of national origin to enforce US immigration law because it would disproportionately impact non-US persons. But the absurdity of that position was too much even for the hare-brained equity obsessives to swallow.

So instead, the DoJ sued Texas under the 1899 Rivers and Harbors Act, arguing that floating barbed-wire barriers in the middle of the Rio Grande obstruct a navigable waterway without the consent of Congress. The 1899 act forbids "build[ing] or commenc[ing] the building of any wharf, pier, dolphin, boom, weir, breakwater, bulkhead, jetty, or other structures in any port, roadstead, haven, harbor, canal, navigable river, or other water of the United States, outside established harbor lines, or where no harbor lines have been established, except on plans recommended by the Chief of Engineers and authorized by the Secretary of the Army."

The extreme Left is adept at this kind of thing, abusing the legal process to hurt America. The case is still going back and forth among the courts.

In the meantime, the federal government is doing everything it can to destroy the border and ease the entry of as many migrants as possible. And when I say "destroy" I am not exaggerating. In March 2024 Judicial Watch filed a Freedom of Information Act lawsuit against the US Department of Homeland Security for all records about Customs and Border Patrol agents welding open "flood gates" in the border wall in Arizona.

In the lawsuit we cited an August 22, 2023, article, in which the US Border Patrol admits it was responsible for a decision to weld open more than 100 "flood gates" in the wall at the US southern border in Arizona, allowing access points for illegal aliens to unlawfully enter the US.

It is hard to express how extraordinary this action is. It's the national equivalent of a bank president welding open the door to the vault, or a prison warden welding open the main gate of the prison. The Border Patrol, under dictate from Washington, is literally undoing the borders of the country.[17]

In a sane society, this would be treason.

The *New York Post's* report cites Border Patrol data showing the border sector at Tucson, which includes the area with the open flood gates, had become the busiest in the country, with the Border Patrol encountering 42,561 individuals trying to cross legally and illegally into the country in July 2023.

The report states: "About 1,400 migrants a day from as far away as China and Egypt as well as Central and South American countries are walking through the open gates, then looking for a Border Patrol agent to surrender to and claim asylum."[18]

"The Biden administration is unlawfully hiding records about literally opening the flood gates for the Biden border invasion," I said at the time.

Of course, that's not the only time the Biden administration has rushed to make America less safe in order to expedite the onrush of illegal immigrants. In October 2022 Judicial Watch revealed that, in response to "a surge of irregular migration," Biden officials were deploying Federal Air Marshals (FAM) to the Mexican border to "protect the life and safety of federal personnel," according to a Department of Homeland Security memo.

Judicial Watch obtained a copy of the directive from various recipients at the agency, which is part of the Transportation Security Administration (TSA), created after 9/11 to prevent another terrorist attack. FAM are charged with protecting commercial passenger flights by deterring and countering the risk of terrorist activity.

The marshals, specially trained aviation security specialists, were outraged that they were being sent to the southern border to provide babysitting services for illegal aliens. Among the duties they would be performing on the southern border were "Hospital Watch, Transportation, Law Enforcement Searches, Entry Control, Security at CBP Facilities and Welfare Checks." Since no commercial passenger planes were hijacked and flown into office buildings since then, I guess the Biden administration can pat themselves on the back for a job well done. Judicial Watch's public education about this abuse and the activism of the marshals themselves eventually led to the marshals being redeployed to where we want them—protecting the flying public.[19]

....

Federal law still prohibits illegal aliens from obtaining certain government services, including food stamps, Medicaid, and federally supported housing programs. But that hasn't stopped many states and localities from doing everything they can to get the new migrants hooked up to the left-wing lifetime dependency machine.

In April 2020, Judicial Watch filed suit in California to stop the state from expending $75 million of taxpayer funds to provide direct cash assistance to unlawfully present aliens. We said that Governor Gavin Newsom overstepped his authority and violated federal law when, without affirmative state legislative approval, he took executive action to create the "Disaster Relief Assistance for Immigrants Project" and provide cash benefits to illegal aliens who otherwise are ineligible for state or federal insurance or other benefits due to their unlawful presence in the United States.

On April 15, 2020, Governor Newsom announced his new executive initiative to provide direct assistance in the form of cash benefits to illegal aliens. The initiative, known as the "Disaster Relief Fund" or the "Disaster Relief Assistance for Immigrants Project," would spend $75 million to provide direct cash payments to illegal aliens and cost an estimated additional $4.8 million to administer. Governor Newsom's executive initiative would provide one-time cash benefits of $500 per adult/$1,000 per household to 150,000 unlawfully present aliens in California. These benefits are not provided to US citizens residing in the state.

According to federal law, state benefits for illegal aliens can only be provided if the state legislature passes a law specifying so. Newsom was acting unilaterally.

"Governor Newsom has no legal authority on his own to spend state taxpayer money for cash payments to illegal aliens," I said at the time. "The coronavirus challenge doesn't give politicians a pass to violate the law. If California politicians want to give cash payments to illegal aliens, they must be accountable and transparent, and, as federal law requires, pass a law to do so."[20]

Naturally enough, a California court refused to stop Newsom from disbursing the money even though it conceded that Judicial Watch was right about the law. But in this case, they ruled, the coronavirus crisis created a "public interest" in ignoring the law and handing out the money anyway.

We filed a similar case in Montgomery County, Maryland, one of the richest, swampiest jurisdictions in America, and a place where "undocumented immigrants" thrive, protected from immigration enforcement. The county planned to hand out $5 million in emergency assistance to illegal aliens, and we sued on behalf of two local residents.

Per usual, a leftist judge denied our suit on the grounds of improper standing. "Whether a federal statute is privately enforceable is up to Congress, not to State courts," the judge wrote. If the court accepted the residents' arguments, "any Maryland taxpayer . . . could challenge any State or local official's actions based on any federal statute, irrespective of the law's relevance to the individual litigant." Heavens forbid!

Of course, these sums are a drop in the bucket compared to what's going on in a place like New York, where the state legislature in 2021 approved a multi-billion-dollar "Excluded Workers Fund." This fund was established to rectify the failure of the federal government to give stimulus checks or extended unemployment benefits to illegal aliens who had worked under the table, and "successfully" handed out the money to over 100,000 illegals. "Qualified" illegal alien applicants got $15,600; "unqualified" applicants, who could provide no evidence that they lost a job due to the pandemic closures, got a consolation award of $3,200.[21]

. . . .

What's the point of all this? Why is an American president, who claims to speak for the working people of the nation, flooding the country with 10 million unvetted foreigners?

On one hand, private interests have always favored mass immigration because it keeps labor costs down. This is a partial explanation of our current economic situation. As Federal Reserve Chairman Jerome Powell explained in congressional testimony in February 2024, "strong job creation has been accompanied by an increase in the supply of workers, particularly among individuals aged twenty-five to fifty-four, and a continued strong pace of immigration."

Low unemployment puts downward pressure on wages. At the same time, inflation has wrecked the consumer's household budget, to the point where people are now spending massively more on groceries, fuel, and housing as a portion of their incomes than they were at the end of Trump's term. This is why proponents of "Bidenomics" are so confused as to why people aren't celebrating what they are being told is a great economy: things may seem fine to economists, but they are terrible for households.

Another reason is described as "votes." Democrats and the Left want more immigrants because immigrants are perceived to be more inclined to vote for Democrat candidates who promise to tax the rich and support their special claims in the distribution of racial spoils.

But, as advocates will chuckle, recent immigrants can't vote! Judicial Watch has demonstrated over the decades that our patchwork electoral system is rife with holes and the potential for abuse, and the potential certainly exists for illegal (and legal) immigrants to vote.

Illegal aliens and noncitizens should not vote in any elections.

It is clear the Left is desperate to allow foreign nationals to vote in our federal elections. They oppose any and all efforts to require proof of citizenship to register to vote and to vote, while promoting alien voting in local elections. In the liberal bastion of Washington, DC, for example, the local politicians have legalized noncitizen voting for mayor, the city council, etc. Now, the law in DC could allow the Russian and Chinese ambassadors (and illegal aliens) to vote and exercise political power in our nation's capital!

Constitutionally speaking, nothing happens in our nation's capital without the sufferance of Congress. That Congress, thanks to the Left and hapless Republican leadership, allows the votes of citizens to be legally stolen by illegal aliens in our nation's capital is reckless and inexcusable.

This points to the more trenchant reason, however, for why the Left wants to open the floodgates and cram as many people into the country as possible. Recall that one of Biden's "Day One" executive orders was to overturn Trump's efforts to exclude illegal aliens from being counted in the census for the purposes of apportioning congressional seats. Flooding Democrat precincts pumps up the population numbers and ensures that concentrated urban areas will retain seats they might otherwise lose.

The most recent reapportionment in Congress resulted in the loss of seats in California, New York, and Pennsylvania, while Florida and Texas gained one and two seats, respectively. New York and California still control a combined 82 electoral votes, which is 30 percent of what a presidential candidate needs to win, but the trend is negative for

Democrats. It is no problem for politicians in "blue" states if socialist policies cause citizens to flee, as they will be replaced with noncitizens who allow those politicians to retain and even increase power.

Congresswoman Yvette Clarke from Brooklyn is a fierce champion of increased immigration, which she praises as the essential value of the American experience. But in a recent Zoom discussion about immigration, Clarke said the quiet part out loud, explaining, "We have a diaspora that can absorb a significant number of these migrants. When I hear colleagues talk about the doors of the inn being closed, 'There's no room at the inn,' I'm saying I need more people in my district just for redistricting purposes."[22]

Forget about the housing crunch, forget about quality of life or school overcrowding. Forget about crime or disorder. Forget about sinking wages. All that matters for Democrat politicians is, ultimately, preserving their districts and increasing political power.

Let me be specific.

To protect our republic, we must shut down the Biden border invasion and deport the illegal aliens ASAP. In addition to undermining our rule of law and sovereignty, their mere presence will ensure increased power for leftist politicians and their allies. If past is prologue, these millions of illegals could help ensure that leftists get dozens of extra seats in Congress (and electors for president) after the next census. Our Congress should answer to American citizens, not invaders from abroad.

Sure enough, all Senate leftist Democrats voted down this year a Senate amendment that "would require that the census determine basic population statistics like the number of citizens, noncitizens, and illegal aliens that live in this country," and it would require that only US citizens be counted in determining the number of House seats and electoral votes that each state gets.

Currently, illegal aliens are counted for determining how many congressional seats and electoral college votes each state gets. This not only destroys the principle of one person, one vote by making some Americans' votes more powerful than others, but it encourages illegal immigration in sanctuary cities as a way to increase political power. The weight of every American's vote should be equal. More illegal alien resettlement shouldn't mean more political power in America.

Is there any doubt the Left seeks, in short, to end America as we have known it?

CHAPTER 2

LAWFARE TARGETING TRUMP

From the beginning of Trump's first presidential campaign in 2015, the Left has treated him and his agenda with total hysteria. No assertion is too wild. He is a fascist, a Nazi, a racist. He wants to enrich himself by selling the nation's secrets to the highest bidder. He was recruited as a Soviet spy in the 1980s. He is a pervert who has raped dozens of women. He wants to subvert democracy just for the sake of doing so. His family is a criminal conspiracy engaged in massive fraud and theft.

As any student of psychology or close observer of human nature will tell you, though, the harshest criticism is often a projection of the critic's own guilty conscience. This has certainly been the case with the Democrats and their leftist allies in the media, as nearly every bad thing they have accused Trump are things they have done.

The trial and conviction of Donald Trump in the New York courts, on picayune charges that made no sense to anyone, with an ethically challenged and compromised judge, based on the testimony of a compulsive liars and criminal, has starkly demonstrated the weaponization of the American system of justice before the law. The regime has declared war on its political enemies, empowering a county prosecutor to gin up ridiculous charges against the leading presidential candidate. If they can do it to him, imagine what they could do to the rest of us?

The motto of Judicial Watch is "No one is above the law," and we have doggedly pursued the matter of corruption across presidential administrations for the last thirty years. In this chapter I want to, briefly, sketch out the extraordinary venality of the Biden family and the work we have done to expose this criminal syndicate to the light of day.

But first we need to talk about the disgusting attack on Trump in the state of New York, its own swamp of corruption. New York, as you well know, is a deep blue state. Most of the Democrats' electoral and financial power in New York derives from New York City, which is effectively run as a one-party state where socialists steer the agenda.

Democrat corruption in New York is not just a term that is tossed around with nothing to back it up. The previous governor, Andrew Cuomo, was forced to resign for having sexually harassed numerous women. The previous elected governor, Eliot Spitzer, resigned after it emerged that he patronized high-end prostitutes and structured his payments to avoid bank reporting laws. The current governor, Kathy Hochul, has been implicated in multiple pay-to-play schemes involving the selling of licenses and franchises, though she has not been indicted, yet.

The previous attorney general, Eric Schneiderman, resigned after it was revealed that he had a penchant for beating up his romantic partners as part of what he called "role-playing." Anthony Weiner, a US congressman and leading candidate for mayor, went to prison for sending naked pictures of himself to a minor. Governor Kathy Hochul's first lieutenant governor, Brian Benjamin, resigned after his federal indictments for bribery and fraud.

The powerful former Speaker of the New York State Assembly, Sheldon Silver, died in federal prison serving a lengthy term for extortion and fraud. Multiple Democrat leaders of the New York State Senate—Pedro Espada, Malcolm Smith, and John Sampson—were convicted of federal corruption charges and went to prison. The previous elected

New York State Comptroller, Alan Hevesi, was convicted of state corruption charges.

And the corruption is bipartisan. Case in point is the disgraced former Republican congressman George Santos, who faces myriad federal corruption charges.

There have been dozens of cases involving elected officials at lower levels of government, but the fish rots from the head down, and this list gives you a whiff of the malodorous garbage can that is New York State politics.

The leading characters in the prosecution of Donald Trump all emerged from this political dung heap. Attorney General Letitia James originally came to elected office after her predecessor was assassinated by an aggrieved opponent. James ran on the ballot line of the far-left Working Families Party—to this date the only person to win without the cross-endorsement of the Democrat Party, though she has since run as a Democrat.

Her campaign for state attorney general in 2018 was based primarily on a promise to investigate Donald Trump. She and her competitors in the primary spent an entire debate describing the methods and techniques they would use to "take on Trump." At this point, there were no allegations that Trump had committed any crimes; James and her fellow Democrats were promising that they would tear apart his business records and find crimes to prosecute him for.

This is not justice. It is persecution. As Stalin's secret police chief Lavrentiy Beria said, "Show me the man and I will find you the crime." This is the essence of totalitarianism, where the government goes out sniffing for violations committed by political enemies. And that has been the basis of all the prosecution of Trump that has taken place in New York.

Letitia James couldn't find any criminal charges to use to go after Trump, so she concocted a civil case against him for having overvalued certain properties in applying for loans from major commercial banks. The banks in question performed their own due diligence before approving their loans, and they were paid back in full, plus interest. So there were no complaints, and no one lost money.

But James brought suit against Trump for fraud, and Democratic Judge Arthur Engoron sided with her argument, finding that Trump had, for example, overvalued Mar-a-Lago by hundreds of millions of dollars. But Engoron applied the local Palm Beach County tax assessor's limited valuation of the massive estate, even though the tax assessment was specifically calculated at a fraction of market value. And so Engoron arbitrarily fined Trump hundreds of millions of dollars for what many real estate investors describe as a routine practice.

It's worth noting that New York State is the only state in the country where most judges are hand-selected by county bosses before appearing on the ballot for election. State supreme court judges—who handle criminal and other serious cases—are named by the local heads of the party, and the party endorsements are handed out as patronage plums. This is a holdover from the days when Tammany Hall ran New York City, and unlike every other jurisdiction in America, most New York judges today are political hacks, not neutral jurists. Engoron has certainly proven himself in the first category.

That was the first of several cases brought against Trump in New York. And they only get more absurd.

In 2019, while Trump was still president, E. Jean Carroll, a former magazine columnist, came forward and said that she had been raped by him in Bergdorf Goodman, an expensive department store near Trump Tower. She said she wasn't sure when it happened, but that it was some time in the mid-1990s. She claimed that she bumped into Trump in the lobby of the store, they started talking, and then he raped her in the women's intimate apparel department.

Trump denied knowing Carroll, much less having raped her. She sued him for defamation, claiming that his denial of her claim had be-smirched her reputation. You'd think that anyone is entitled to defend themselves by denying guilt for something they are accused of. But in the mirror world of the New York court system, saying that you are falsely accused means you are calling your accuser a liar.

E. Jean Carroll's lawyer, Roberta Kaplan, is a major player in na-tional Democrat politics with deep ties to Hillary Clinton and the Obamas. She gained Democrat superstardom as the lawyer for Edith Windsor, whose case before the Supreme Court resulted in the legaliza-tion of gay marriage. Kaplan co-founded Time's Up, the legal advocacy group for women suing over sexual harassment, but had to resign in 2021 when it emerged that she was helping Andrew Cuomo with his own sexual harassment charges.

Roberta Kaplan worked with the New York State legislature—which had a Democrat supermajority—to enact the Adult Survivors Act, a law that allowed victims of sexual offenses for which the statute of limitations had expired to file civil suits against their assailants. The law would provide a brief one-year window in which to file suits. It was widely understood that the ASA was meant to get Trump.

E. Jean Carroll sued Trump for raping her and for defamation, and the two suits were combined as one. There was no direct evidence offered except for Carroll's hazy testimony that it happened. The jury found that Trump had sexually assaulted Carroll and awarded her $5 million in damages. Because Trump continued to deny the charge, and insinuated that Carroll was lying, she sued him for defamation again. This time Trump was ordered to pay Carroll an additional $83.3 million.

In 2021, Manhattan District Attorney Alvin Bragg was elected to office—with massive financial support from George Soros—on the promise that he would not prosecute "minor" crimes such as trespass-ing or resisting arrest. He also swore that he would operate under a presumption of non-incarceration for almost all crimes except the most serious. Bragg boasted about his experience suing the Trump administration "more than 100 times" and campaigned on a platform of "holding [Trump] accountable."

Bragg inherited a moribund investigation into Trump from Cy Vance, the previous district attorney, and initially indicated he had no interest in pursuing it. The investigation concerned money that Trump had paid, through his former attorney Michael Cohen, to a woman called Stormy Daniels with whom he had allegedly had sex. The question concerning the money was if it could be considered a campaign expenditure. The Federal Election Commission and anti-Trump Justice Department prosecutors had already looked into the matter and found no crimes. Cy Vance hadn't made anything of it, either.

But Bragg came under pressure after high-profile prosecutors, including Mark Pomerantz, who had come out of retirement specifically to go after Trump, went public with their dissatisfaction that Bragg was dropping the ball. Michael Colangelo, the number three man in the Biden Justice Department and a former senior Obama official, was seemingly sent to New York first to oversee Letitia James's case, and then hired by Bragg to work as the point man there.

Bragg's case against Trump was tendentious and flimsy. It broke new legal ground in the rules of evidence and procedure. Judge Juan Merchan refused to recuse himself even though he had made political contributions earmarked to oppose Trump, his wife was until recently an employee of New York State Attorney General Letitia James, and his daughter Loren Merchan is a significant Democrat fundraiser for avowed enemies of Trump. Among Loren Merchan's clients are Adam Schiff, the California congressman who established himself as Trump's scourge during the Russiagate investigation.

Another client of Loren Merchan is Dan Goldman, currently a congressman from Manhattan. Before his election to Congress, Goldman served as lead majority counsel in the first impeachment inquiry against Donald Trump and lead counsel to the House Managers in Trump's second impeachment trial. In Congress he plays the role of bulldog, ferociously attacking anyone who dares question the probity of the Biden family. Goldman has attained legendary status for his persistent claim that the famous laptop that Hunter Biden abandoned in a computer store is a Russian hoax.

So Judge Merchan has deep ties to the Democrat party, and that's especially relevant given the details of the case. Bragg's case rested on the novel argument that internal business records that no one would ever see in the normal course of events were falsely labeled as "legal expenses," though they were in fact records of payments made to an attorney. This alleged falsification—a misdemeanor that had already passed the statute of limitations—was revived by tying it to the furtherance of another crime. This underlying crime, a state elections law, is also a misdemeanor that had passed the statute of limitations. But under Bragg's magical argument, two expired misdemeanors combined together are a felony!

The number of obviously reversible errors in this case form a mountain, and I'm not going to go through them here because they have already been discussed thoroughly in other venues by legal experts. Many have no doubt that the ridiculous verdict will be overturned on appeal. But the New York court process first allowed a ridiculous and innocent set of facts to be used to obtain a ridiculous indictment followed by a ridiculous trial, so I am a bit skeptical that Trump will be completely (or timely) exonerated in the Empire State's courts. Even if he is exonerated, the whole point of the case was to brand Trump as a "felon" in the run-up to the 2024 election. Alex Soros, whose father's contributions helped install Bragg as DA, wrote, "Democrats should refer to Trump as a convicted felon at every opportunity. Repetition is the key to a successful message and we want people to wrestle with the notion of hiring a convicted felon for the most important job in the country!"[1]

Judicial Watch kept a close eye on the case and on Alvin Bragg in particular. In 2023, Congressman Jim Jordan, the chair of the House Judiciary Committee, subpoenaed Mark Pomerantz to speak in closed-door testimony about Bragg's investigation of Trump, the extent to which it had used federal funds, and how it represented a significant weaponization of the judicial system for political ends. "It now appears," wrote Jordan, "that your efforts to shame Bragg have worked as he is reportedly resurrecting a so-called 'zombie' case against President Trump using a tenuous and untested legal theory. Even the *Washington Post* quoted 'legal experts' as calling Bragg's actions 'unusual' because 'prosecutors have repeatedly examined the long-established details but decided not to pursue charges.'"

Pomerantz refused to appear before the Judiciary Committee, and Bragg sued Jordan, claiming that his subpoena was "an unconstitutional attempt to undermine an ongoing New York felony criminal prosecution and investigation." A federal judge eventually sided with Jordan, and Pomerantz was obliged to sit for a deposition with the committee.

We filed a Freedom of Information Request from Bragg's office for information regarding its contract with Gibson, Dunn & Crutcher LLP, one of the largest law firms in the world, to help Bragg with his issues with Jim Jordan. After some hemming and hawing, Bragg's office eventually turned over a retainer agreement.

The letter welcomes "the Manhattan District Attorney's Office ('the DA') as a client of Gibson, Dunn & Crutcher LLP . . . You are retaining us to provide legal services to the DA in connection with a congressional investigation, potential litigation, and related matters regarding the DA's investigation of Donald Trump (the 'Matter')."

Initially redacted in its first production of records, the "professional fees" section states: "For this matter we have agreed on the following hourly rates for our attorneys: $900 per hour for partners, and $500 per hour for associates. These rates will remain the same for the life of the matter."

"Bragg's unjustified, malicious prosecution is not only corrupt but it's also a waste of taxpayer funds as he tries to thwart a legitimate House investigation into his attempt to interfere in the 2024 election," I said at the time. "Rather than spending $900 per hour on lawyers to defend his abuse of office and political jihad against Trump, Bragg should focus on taking dangerous criminals off the streets of New York."[2]

Trump's conviction in the Bragg trial evolves around the question of a payout that was supposedly mislabeled as "legal fees." It's worth noting that in the 2016 election cycle, the Hillary Clinton campaign hired Fusion GPS to concoct the Steele dossier—the infamous document alleging that Donald Trump and his campaign were actively colluding with Russian agents to subvert the presidential election and install Trump as an illegitimate ruler.

The Steele dossier was leaked to the FBI and served as the basis for the FISA warrants that led to the entire Mueller investigation, which hamstrung the Trump administration for years, cost millions of dollars, and destroyed lives.

In 2022, the Hillary Clinton campaign and the Democratic National Committee quietly agreed to pay more than $100,000 in fines to the Federal Election Commission pertaining to the 2016 election. What was the problem? It turns out that the Clinton campaign used its law firm, Perkins Coie, to handle its negotiations with Fusion GPS. Perkins Coie was paid millions by the Clinton campaign, and paid the campaign's bill to Fusion GPS for its hard work coming up with the hoax about Trump colluding with Putin.

But when the Clinton campaign filed its paperwork with the FEC, it never specified that the payments were campaign related. Instead, they were listed as "legal expenses." That is to say, Hillary Clinton actually did exactly what Donald Trump was accused of doing, but didn't. But in her case, nobody sought to concoct an elaborate criminal prosecution; they just dinged her campaign and the DNC with a piddling fine.

Unequal justice is the essence of totalitarianism. As Óscar Benavides, the one-time president of Peru, said, "For my friends, everything; for my enemies, the law."

....

The second of four criminal indictments against Trump, brought in Fulton County, Georgia, alleges that he and more than a dozen co-defendants conspired to steal the 2020 election and defraud the voters of Georgia. With forty-one counts subsumed under the state Racketeer Influenced and Corrupt Organizations (RICO) law, the prosecution held that

> Defendant Donald John Trump lost the United States presidential election held on November 3, 2020. One of the states he lost was Georgia. Trump and the other Defendants charged in this Indictment refused to accept that Trump lost, and they knowingly and willfully joined a conspiracy to unlawfully change the outcome of the election in favor of Trump. That conspiracy contained a common plan and purpose to commit two or more acts of racketeering activity in Fulton County, Georgia, elsewhere in the State of Georgia, and in other states.

This case is a pure example of the criminalization of politics. It alleges that, as the first "Act" of the conspiracy, that "on or about the 4th day of November 2020, DONALD JOHN TRUMP made a nationally televised speech falsely declaring victory in the 2020 presidential election." November 4 was the day after Election Day, when the votes had not been counted yet and the election results were still in question. Candidates for office frequently declare "victory" before it's official; saying that it's a crime to do so or an effort to steal an election is ridiculous.

As an aside, note that the anti-Trump media refers constantly to how Trump "falsely" said something, or that he "lied," even when he is giving an opinion about something. So-called fact checkers claim that Trump has "lied" tens of thousands of times, and the *Washington Post* even maintains a database detailing each of his 30,573 "false or misleading claims" throughout his presidency. "On Nov. 2 alone, the day before the 2020 vote, Trump made 503 false or misleading claims as he barnstormed across the country in a desperate effort to win re-election."[3]

But the lies that the *Post* alleges Trump to have made include his claim that his wife, Melania, "has been a woman of great grace and beauty and dignity. And so popular with the people, so popular with the people." According to the *Post*'s fact checkers, Melania was not popular. Another time, Trump said, "I don't care about Twitter. Twitter's bad news." The *Post* made another notch on its tally of lies and pointed out that Trump in fact enjoyed using Twitter. You can see from all this why leftist fact-checking is essentially juvenile.

The national discourse, driven by media repetition, has hammered on the theme that Trump is an inveterate liar. But when you look at how the press has treated Trump's successor, you see a completely different approach. Though Joe Biden confabulates constantly—such as claiming to have been recruited to play football at the Naval Academy; or to have been arrested in South Africa when going to visit Nelson Mandela in prison; or that his son died in combat in Iraq; or that he was the first person in his family to go to college—fact checkers rarely cite his fictions, and even when they do, they never assimilate his lies into a general depiction of his character, as they do with Trump.

A key element of the RICO case against Trump in Fulton County surrounds a conversation he had with Georgia Secretary of State Brad Raffensperger, in which the president asked Raffensperger, who was conducting a ballot audit in Cobb County, to do a diligent count as only "11,780 votes" separated Trump and Biden. This was taken by the media, and Fulton County District Attorney Fani Willis, as evidence that Trump was demanding that Raffensperger overturn the election or falsify the ballot count. But in actuality, it is not uncommon in close elections for candidates and their attorneys to run aggressive campaigns during the vote count to "find" votes. Simply put, the closeness of the election demanded a diligent analysis of the votes.

As I described in an earlier chapter, the 2020 election was highly irregular and unlike any previous election. Massive numbers of mail-in ballots overwhelmed election staff, and accepted standards of legibility of signatures, postmarks, witnessing, and marking of ballots were largely neglected. So raising questions about ballot integrity was hardly bizarre, or illegal. In any case, those charges were quashed by Judge Scott McAfee in March 2024, after he determined that the claim that the defendants "violated their oaths" to the Constitution were too broad to prosecute.

The entire Georgia case ought to be thrown out. The charges are ridiculous and ignore the constitutional and statutory rights of Trump—as president, citizen, and candidate—the right to pursue a fair count of the ballots. The charges are abusive, because they were generated through the ethical and criminal misconduct of Democratic politician Fani Willis. Willis was praised by the national media in August 2023, when she indicted Trump and many other Republicans, as a heroic prosecutor and a tough-minded expert on conspiracy cases. But the shenanigans in her office soon began a national media circus when it emerged that she hired her married lover Nathan Wade to serve as lead litigator in the case.

Wade was paid a generous salary, approved by Willis, to manage the case against Trump, and the couple went on extravagant vacations together, which Wade appeared to have paid for. The evident corruption—or at least the appearance of impropriety—was so manifest that Judge McAfee ruled that Wade must leave the case. Meanwhile, the Georgia legislature is investigating Willis, who appears to have lied under oath. Judge McAfee did let Willis and her office remain on the case, though he permitted Trump to pursue appeals to knock Willis off the prosecution as well.

Just as the Biden administration appears to have meddled with the two New York cases against Trump, by "assigning" a top Justice Department official to work for Tish James and Alvin Bragg, it seems likely that the White House and its congressional allies "managed" with the Georgia case, too. Fani Willis went to the White House and met with Kamala Harris in February 2023, according to the White House visitors logs; the visit may have only been part of a gathering of black elected officials as part of Black History Month, but neither Willis nor the vice president have offered any details about their interactions that day.

Judicial Watch sued the Fulton County District Attorney's office to obtain any communications that Fani Willis may have had with either the office of Special Counsel Jack Smith—who was heading up a federal investigation of Donald Trump—or with the Pelosi House January 6 Committee. Willis's office claimed in response to our original request to have no such documentation, but she evidently lied. Representative Jim Jordan discovered a letter from Fani Willis to Congressman Bennie Thompson, the Democrat Chair of the January 6 Committee, dated December 17, 2021, requesting a meeting with Thompson and access to the committee's files. The letter read in part:

Dear Chairman Thompson:

As you may be aware, I am conducting a criminal investigation of possible attempts to illegally interfere with the administration of Georgia's 2020 General Election. Through news reports, we are aware that your committee has interviewed witnesses relevant to our investigation.

We understand from the same reports that your committee's investigators may have collected records relevant to our investigation. Please accept this letter as an official request from me for access to records that may be relevant to our criminal investigation. Those record include but are not limited to recordings and transcripts of witness interviews and depositions, electronic and print records of communications, and records of travel.

It may well be most efficient for your staff and effective for our understanding for my staff and me to meet with your Investigators in person. We are able to travel to Washington any time between January 31, 2022 and February 25, 2022. We will do our best to accommodate the schedule of the committee.[4]

Given Willis's failure to provide even this letter of inquiry in response to the Judicial Watch request, it remains an open question as to how much coordination may have taken place between the office of the Fulton County District Attorney and federal officials in regard to the massive RICO indictment of Donald Trump. But given the rank dishonesty, open conflicts of interests, and naked financial corruption that appears to have directed the actions of her office, who would be surprised if she was holding back information about a conspiracy against Trump from the highest levels of the United States government?

Jack Smith, the special counsel prosecuting Donald Trump, was appointed to his position by Biden's Attorney General Merrick Garland in November 2022, three days after Trump announced he would seek election to his former office. The timing was no coincidence. Every aspect of the prosecution of Donald Trump has been weaponized law-fare against a political opponent, the sort of thing we expect to find in corrupt Third World countries.

Smith has a history of prosecuting political corruption, and was the lead in taking down Virginia governor Bob McDonnell, a Republican, on corruption charges. This case, however, wound up being overturned *unanimously* by the Supreme Court, and it established a new precedent in bribery and public corruption law. The court threw out the conviction of McDonnell, who had sponsored an event for a tobacco company after getting a gift from the company's CEO, ruling that convicting a public official of bribery requires a very specific and narrow quid pro quo. Iron-ically, the Court's ruling in *McDonnell v. United States* may emerge as relevant in Trump's appeal of his conviction in the Bragg case.

Trump faces two federal criminal indictments thanks to Smith. The first, filed in the DC courts, is an echo of Fani Willis's indictment and asserts that Trump, while president, engaged in a "conspiracy to de-fraud the United States," as well as a "conspiracy to obstruct an official proceeding." Essentially, this case alleges that Trump's actions on and leading up to January 6 were a conscious effort to seize control of the government and stay in office. Smith contends:

The Defendant, DONALD J. TRUMP, was the forty-fifth President of the United States and a candidate for re-election in 2020. The Defendant lost the 2020 presidential election.

Despite having lost, the Defendant was determined to remain in power. So for more than two months following election day on November 3, 2020, the Defendant spread lies that there had been outcome-determinative fraud in the election and that he had actually won. These claims were false, and the Defendant knew that they were false. But the Defendant repeated and widely disseminated them anyway—

to make his knowingly false claims appear legitimate, create an intense national atmosphere of mistrust and anger, and erode public faith in the administration of the election.

The idea that making "false claims" about a political event is a crime is absurd. And Smith, in a concession to Trump's right to speak freely, acknowledges that

The Defendant had a right, like every American, to speak publicly about the election and even to claim, falsely, that there had been outcome-determinative fraud during the election and that he had won. He was also entitled to formally challenge the results of the election through lawful and appropriate means, such as by seeking recounts or audits of the popular vote in states or filing lawsuits challenging ballots and procedures.

Nevertheless, Smith's indictment insists that Trump engaged in a criminal conspiracy to disrupt American democracy by pursuing claims of electoral fraud in several states where the vote was close, and by entertaining legal theories about how Congress and the vice president are supposed to determine the winner of a presidential election.

The indictment is filled with references to "false claims." Smith charges, for instance, "the Defendant widely disseminated his false claims of election fraud for months, despite the fact that he knew, and in many cases had been informed directly, that they were not true. The Defendant's knowingly false statements were integral to his criminal plans to defeat the federal government function, obstruct the certification, and interfere with others' right to vote and have their votes counted. He made these knowingly false claims throughout the post-election time period . . ."[5]

The indictment reads as if an anti-Trump fact checker was suddenly given prosecutorial power!

The question of a sitting president pursuing options or alternatives, or of asking public officials to consider the possibility that the votes in their jurisdictions were subject to fraud, may be unconventional in American political history, but recall the bizarre conditions under which the 2020 election was held. There is no question that the rapid application of new balloting regulations were handled illegally, because they were ordered by judges, secretaries of state, or governors, not by state legislatures as the Constitution specifies. Ballot collection and inspection were performed in an ad hoc manner. It was reasonable for a losing candidate to explore all possible remedies following a close election held under these circumstances.

Let's not forget how the Democrats behaved after the 2016 election, either. Hillary Clinton has yet to acknowledge that she lost. There are viral videos of leading Democrat officials calling Trump's election "stolen" and insisting that he was an "illegitimate" president. It is clear that the Obama administration approved wiretapping of the Trump campaign under the knowingly fictitious allegation that Trump was working with Russia to steal the election, a charge that was ginned up by the Clinton campaign.

In August 2020, prior to the election, Hillary Clinton stated, "Joe Biden should not concede under any circumstances because I think this is going to drag out, and eventually I do believe he will win if we don't give an inch and if we are as focused and relentless as the other side is." According to this advice, the Biden campaign was prepared to fight as sneakily and aggressively as possible.

The Democrats have contested every Republican presidential victory since 2000. They called George W. Bush the "selected president" because of the 2000 *Bush v. Gore* Supreme Court decision that an extended ballot count in certain Florida counties would violate the Equal

Protection Clause of the Constitution, thus forcing Florida to cast its electoral votes for Bush. In 2004, the election turned on Ohio, and Democrats claimed—and many still claim—that the voting machines in use were rigged in Bush's favor.

At the end of June, 2024 the Supreme Court issued a major decision ruling that presidents are immune from prosecution for "official acts" undertaken while occupying the White House. As of this writing, we are waiting to see how this ruling will be applied regarding the cases against Trump. The New York case may be thrown out entirely, as might the federal case regarding January 6. The question of presidential immunity is immensely tricky and it will be years before the ramifications of the decision are understood. But the Biden administration has certainly broken new constitutional ground to try to jail Trump, and basically demanded that the Supreme Court step in. The Left can only blame itself for opening this can of worms.

Though the case has been dismissed, and will likely be resolved in the future by the Supreme Court, the last criminal indictment confronting Donald Trump is the most ridiculous one of all. The government claims that Trump, upon leaving the White House, stole classified documents and brought them to Mar-a-Lago, where he lived. "The classified documents TRUMP stored in his boxes included information regarding defense and weapons capabilities of both the United States and foreign countries; United States nuclear programs; potential vulnerabilities of the United States and its allies to military attack; and plans for possible retaliation in response to a foreign attack," read the indictment. "The unauthorized disclosure of these classified documents could put at risk the national security of the United States, foreign relations, the safety of the United States military, and human sources and the continued viability of sensitive intelligence collection methods."

In other words, Trump was putting the nation's security at risk.

To maximize the negative publicity for Trump and compound the appearance of criminality, the Biden Justice Department ordered the FBI to enforce a subpoena with an unprecedented raid of Mar-a-Lago, searching through the bedrooms of the former First Lady and Trump's son Barron. The FBI leaked photos of document folders marked "Top Secret," many of which were empty. Even the "Top Secret" markings were from place holder sheets inserted by the FBI. Occupy Democrats, a far left social media organization with ties to the DNC, has steadily pushed the line that the empty folders are evidence that Trump sold America's secrets to Russia.

Before the indictment, Donald Trump's office was involved in negotiations with the National Archives regarding the disposition of his papers. There was some back and forth regarding what belonged where. As Jack Smith's indictment says,

> As a result of TRUMP's retention of classified documents
> after his presidency and refusal to return them, hundreds of
> classified documents were not recovered by the United States
> government until 2022, as follows:
> a. On January 17, nearly one year after TRUMP left office,
> and after months of demands by the National Archives and
> Records Administration for TRUMP to provide all missing
> presidential records, TRUMP provided only 15 boxes, which
> contained 197 documents with classification markings . . . [6]

This sounds bad—the National Archives had demanded presidential records and Trump wouldn't turn them over. Except the Justice Department changed its legal position in suddenly deciding that Trump had an obligation to turn over his papers from his White House days to the Archivist, who has no authority to make demands of the former chief executive as to which papers were his personal records or not.

Judicial Watch knows this better than anyone, because we were on the losing side of the case that set the standard. Bill Clinton met with writer Taylor Branch seventy-nine times during his administration and recorded the conversations for Clinton's future memoir. As my colleague Michael Bekesha wrote in the *Wall Street Journal*:

> the audiotapes preserved not only Mr. Clinton's thoughts on issues he faced while president, but also some actual events, such as phone conversations. Among them:

- Mr. Clinton calling several U.S. senators and trying to persuade them to vote against an amendment by Sen. John McCain requiring the immediate withdrawal of troops from Somalia.
- Mr. Clinton's side of a phone call with Rep. William Natcher (D., Ky.) in which the president explained that his reasoning for joining the North American Free Trade Agreement was based on technical forecasts in his presidential briefings.
- Mr. Clinton's side of a phone conversation with Secretary of State Warren Christopher about a diplomatic impasse over Bosnia.
- Mr. Clinton seeking advice from Mr. Branch on pending foreign-policy decisions such as military involvement in Haiti and possibly easing the embargo of Cuba.

These recordings captured significant moments in diplomacy and domestic affairs. The conversations took place in the White House. The meetings were arranged by a public employee, who was involved in the logistics of the recordings. Shouldn't they have been available to the public as public records?

This case became known as the "Sock Drawer Case" because of where Clinton stashed the tapes. And the precedent it set established that presidents have pretty much unlimited authority to decide what they want to keep from their time in office. Judicial Watch, dedicated to the openness of government records, fought like hell to get those tapes, but we couldn't. According to the law, they were his property, and there was nothing we could do about it.

Michael concludes:

> The same is true with Mr. Trump. Although he didn't keep records in his sock drawer, he gathered newspapers, press clippings, letters, notes, cards, photographs, documents and other materials in cardboard boxes. Then Mr. Trump, like Mr. Clinton, took those boxes with him when he left office. As of noon on Jan. 20, 2021, whatever remained at the White House was presidential records. Whatever was taken by Mr. Trump wasn't. That was the position of the Justice Department in 2010 and the ruling by Judge Jackson in 2012.
>
> A decade later, the government should never have gone searching for potential presidential records. Nor should it have forcibly taken records from Mr. Trump. The government should lose *U.S. v. Trump.* If the courts decide otherwise, I want those Clinton tapes.[7]

Are we to believe that Barack Obama was subject to the same kind of badgering and scrutiny regarding his papers that Trump was? Seems implausible. And how are we to know what a former president has or doesn't have in his possession, short of sending the FBI in to paw through his wife's clothes closet?

In any event, it turned out that President Biden had kept a lot of classified papers from his decades as a US senator, and his two terms as vice president. Many of them were stacked in his garage in Delaware;

others he showed to a ghostwriter who was working on his memoirs. The FBI did eventually go to his house to retrieve the documents, but only after giving him plenty of time to prepare.

A special counsel, Robert Hur, was assigned to investigate Biden's willful and knowing retention of classified documents. Hur notoriously recommended against charging Biden with any crimes, largely because his poor memory and feebleminded affect would certainly have led a jury to acquit him. But Hur also noted that Biden had the plausible defense that he fairly thought, given prior practice and law, that he had a right to keep any documents he had from his days as vice president. In a stunning display of corrupt selective prosecution, the Justice Department pretends that Trump does not have the defense they using as an excuse not to prosecute Biden.

It is amazing to witness such blatant selective prosecution occurring before our eyes. But that's the reality of America today. "For my friends, everything. For my enemies, the law."

Judicial Watch and I are also victims of this abuse. For blowing the whistle on this unmoored prosecution of Trump over documents and for daring to question the 2020 election, we were retaliated against with grand jury subpoenas.

As I told conservatives in a major speech to the Conservative Political Action Conference, here's what happened:

Not too long ago [November 2022], I had significant skin cancer surgery and a few hours after I got home, I'm on the couch recovering when the FBI comes knocking on my door with a grand jury subpoena from the Biden DOJ. The agents tried to be pleasant and helpfully pointed out that something had come for me from Amazon. I suspect I am the first person in American history to receive FBI notice of an Amazon package delivery.

I ended up being hassled and abused by the Special
Counsel team for four hours over Trump documents, my First
Amendment rights and what I had for lunch at the White
House. It was a partisan fishing expedition.

Frankly, it was like having to spend an entire day on a
MSNBC panel. I knew why they brought me before that grand
jury: it was payback and intimidation for daring to defend
Trump against their abuse of power![6]

Judicial Watch ended up spending significant resources to comply with and fight these subpoenas—and we were only a "witness,"
not a target of the Jack Smith operation! This is a Justice Department
that casually forces the head of America's largest government watchdog organization to testify about our anti-corruption work—targeting
the Justice Department! Imagine the media uproar if the heads of the
ACLU or the NAACP were similarly abused. In today's America, the
civil rights of any American—from Trump to the head of a watchdog
group—can be trampled on by abusers in government.

....

The Left enjoys talking about Donald Trump's family in repulsive
terms. His sons Donald Jr. and Eric are routinely described as gun-
crazy drug addicts and criminals who make money by exploiting their
family name. Trump's relations with his daughter Ivanka are discussed
by nasty media opponents in vulgar terms. Psychologists could have a
field day with the blatant projection. Everything said about Trump and
his family applies precisely to the Bidens, specifically Hunter.

Hunter Biden's entire career has been built around his status as
the son of a powerful senator. After law school he went to work for
the major Delaware bank holding company MBNA, the employees
of which were major contributors to his dad's campaigns. Within two

years he was executive vice president. Then he went to work for the Clinton Department of Commerce, after which—with a total of four years of professional experience—he started his own lobbying company. He was appointed vice chairman of the board of Amtrak—his father's favorite mode of transportation—in 2006, despite having no experience in the transportation industry.

When his father became Obama's vice president in 2009, Hunter put aside lobbying, and he and his uncle James became international financiers and consultants, with extensive interests in Chinese financial and energy companies. In 2013, Hunter flew to China with his father on Air Force Two and met the CEO of BHR Partners, a Shanghai-based investment company that does extensive business with Chinese state-owned firms. Hunter then became a significant owner and board member of BHR. In other words, Hunter was a deal maker working in partnership with "cut-outs" representing the Chinese Communist government.

In 2014, Hunter Biden also became a board member of Burisma Holdings, a Ukrainian energy company, for which he was paid hundreds of thousands of dollars per year. Hunter had no experience in Ukraine or in the energy sector, but his father was managing the Obama administration's Ukrainian policy at the time. Joe Biden bragged openly about telling the Ukrainian president that if a prosecutor who was investigating Burisma wasn't fired immediately, he would block significant loan guarantees from the United States.

Throughout this time, Hunter Biden was also a serious drug addict. A disturbing *New Yorker* magazine profile in 2019 detailed how Hunter would hang out in a tent in Skid Row in Los Angeles, buying crack cocaine and dallying with a woman named Bicycles. Hunter said that finding crack in any city was his "superpower"; nobody told him that crack dealers aren't exactly discreet or especially exclusive.

It was revealed in October 2020, just before the election, that Hunt-

er's laptop and an external hard drive, containing more than 200 giga-
bytes of personal photos, videos, emails, and documents, had been
abandoned by its owner at a Delaware computer repair shop in April
2019. The owner of the shop informed the FBI about the laptop when
he noticed it contained references to "criminality . . . related to foreign
business dealings, to potential money laundering and, more importantly, national security issues and concerns." The FBI seized the laptop
in December 2019.

The owner of the shop, John Paul Mac Isaac, had made a copy
of the laptop's hard drive after nobody came to pick it up. Legally, it
became the property of the shopkeeper after a certain amount of time
had elapsed. Mac Isaac contacted Rudy Giuliani, who gave a copy of
the hard drive to the *New York Post*, which published the contents of
the laptop, including lurid pictures of Hunter Biden naked, having sex
with prostitutes, doing drugs, and discussing his father's involvement
in his business interests, including a notorious 2017 email that mentioned reserving 10 percent of a major deal for "the big guy."

The exposure of the laptop was explosive. It threatened to rock the
presidential election. Here was evidence that Joe Biden did not, as he
always claimed, have no interest or even knowledge of his son's business, but he was in fact deeply entwined with it. Hunter Biden traveled
frequently with his father on Air Force Two. Joe Biden frequently met
Hunter's potential foreign national business partners, dropping by at
the end of dinners to say hello. The entire Biden family was getting
rich as consultants, advisors, and strategists, but it was never clear what
any of them *did*. It was a family business, and the only product was
access—real or perceived—to Joe Biden.

The complex business dealings of the Biden family have been detailed elsewhere, and I don't mean to spend a lot of time on it here.
It's all documented. What I want to focus on is the combined and
total response of the "deep state"—the media, government, and "in-

telligence community"—to the introduction of the laptop to the news cycle. They behaved as an immune system responds to a virus, with an all-hands mission-critical smothering of the foreign body.

The first *Post* story about the laptop, on October 14, 2020, published an email from Vadym Pozharskyi, a Burisma executive. As the *Post* reported:

> Hunter Biden introduced his father, then-Vice President Joe Biden, to a top executive at a Ukrainian energy firm less than a year before the elder Biden pressured government officials in Ukraine into firing a prosecutor who was investigating the company, according to emails obtained by *The Post*.
>
> The never-before-revealed meeting is mentioned in a message of appreciation that Vadym Pozharskyi, an adviser to the board of Burisma, allegedly sent Hunter Biden on April 17, 2015, about a year after Hunter joined the Burisma board at a reported salary of up to $50,000 a month.
>
> "Dear Hunter, thank you for inviting me to DC and giving an opportunity to meet your father and spent [*sic*] some time together. It's realty [*sic*] an honor and pleasure," the email reads.
>
> An earlier email from May 2014 also shows Pozharskyi, reportedly Burisma's No. 3 exec, asking Hunter for "advice on how you could use your influence" on the company's behalf.[9]

The *Post*'s reporting was immediately and furiously denounced as a Russian disinformation ploy. Within a few days, more than fifty members of the "intelligence community," including former directors and acting directors of the CIA, the DIA, the NSA, the NIA, the DOD, etc., signed a letter asserting that the laptop was, in all likelihood, a setup. Admitting that they hadn't seen the laptop and knew nothing about it except what they read in the papers, the signatories, using their credentials, explained that it "has all the classic earmarks of a Russian information operation."

Three days later, Joe Biden debated President Trump on national television. He cited the "intelligence community" letter as evidence that Trump was using Russian disinformation to defame him. "There are fifty former national intelligence folks who said that what he's accusing me of is a Russian plant," Biden insisted.

Major social media companies, including Twitter and Facebook, rushed to block references to the laptop story. The *New York Post* Twitter account was suspended, and Twitter did not permit users to link to the story or even share it through direct messages. National Public Radio called the story a "waste of time" and a "distraction."

The mass suppression of the laptop story is particularly bizarre because the laptop has since been acknowledged as completely legitimate. Everything on it belonged to Hunter Biden and all the emails were valid emails sent by the senders identified in the headings. During Hunter Biden's trial in June 2024 on federal gun charges, the Biden Department of Justice entered the laptop as evidence, and an FBI forensic specialist testified that the laptop was not tampered with.

But the campaign to denigrate the laptop as a Russian ploy and to vilify the Trump campaign for amplifying Russian disinformation was not simply a matter of political bias or a rush to judgment. Rather, the entire process was orchestrated as a rapid response tactic by Joe Biden's political campaign. The 2023 House Committee on the Judiciary, Select Subcommittee on the Weaponization of the Federal Government, and Permanent Select Committee on Intelligence report on the now-infamous statement detailed specifically how Biden campaign advisor Anthony Blinken, the future secretary of state, solicited the letter from former CIA acting director Michael Morell, who later testified that without Blinken's urging, the letter never would have been written or disseminated.

Morell testified that the letter was specifically written to "help Vice President Biden in the debate." As the House report states: "Indeed, some of the former intelligence officials who signed the public statement were deeply satisfied that Vice President Biden referred to the statement in the final presidential debate before the election. After the debate, the signers congratulated themselves on a job well done, and the Biden campaign even called to thank Morell for organizing the effort."

The suppression of the story on Twitter, as shown in the "Twitter Files" that were released after Elon Musk's acquisition of the company, reveals that top Twitter executives rushed to block mention of the laptop as part of a general dynamic wherein Biden campaign staffers routinely asked Twitter to delete objectionable tweets. Matt Taibbi, one of the Twitter Files authors, wrote, "By 2020, requests from connected actors to delete tweets were routine. One executive would write to another: 'More to review from the Biden team.' The reply would come back: 'Handled.'"[10]

The weaponization of the judiciary, the media, the intelligence community, and the law—the "deep state" or the "swamp" as Trump calls it—has become almost total in America. A few areas remain untouched and free. But the Left regime is working in overdrive to drown those few lights of freedom.

There is a storm front of selective, vindictive, political, and anti-constitutional prosecutions going from Miami, through Fulton County, Georgia, here in DC, and up into New York. And the front has expanded to other states where lawyers, Republican party officials, and volunteers are being harassed, sued, disbarred, and prosecuted for exercising their God-given First Amendment and other rights to dispute an election.

Let me be clear: moving to jail the leading presidential candidate, seize his assets, and destroy his business are all about turning America into a one-party state.

CHAPTER 3

DIVERSITY SCAMS AND PARTY SPOILS

The promise of America has always been based on equality. But what is equality? This once was something that was broadly understood and largely agreed upon.

The Declaration of Independence, really our founding document, is like the "mission statement" of our country. It sets out the core values that America seeks to uphold. "We hold these truths to be self-evident," the document explains, "that all men are created equal, that they are endowed by their Creator with certain unalienable Rights, that among these are Life, Liberty and the pursuit of Happiness."

We are "created equal." But anyone can look around and note that we aren't all "equal" in terms of our talents, gifts, height, good looks, smarts, or wealth. In fact, we are all tremendously unequal, and God bless that variety. Imagine if everyone was exactly the same—life would be pretty dull.

The sense in which Thomas Jefferson, the author of our Declaration, meant that "all men are created equal" arrives in the next clause, in which he clarifies that we have all been given certain natural rights by God, including the right to live, to be free, and to pursue happiness. God has created us equal in his eyes, both as members of the human family and as political agents who are capable of self-governance.

America was the first country to be established on the principle that the sovereign power of the nation resides in and with the people. As the Declaration continues, "That to secure these rights, Governments are instituted among Men, deriving their just powers from the consent of the governed." Rights flow from God to the people, who establish governments, and the power of the government flows from the consent of the people.

Heidi Przybyla, a journalist for Politico, went viral in February 2024 for mocking so-called Christian nationalists because, as she condescendingly explained, "They believe that our rights as Americans, as all human beings, do not come from any earthly authority. They don't come from Congress, they don't come from the Supreme Court, they come from God."

This is typical of, and indeed exemplifies, the perspective of the unthinking, communist mentality that predominates among the media, academia, the judiciary, and among leftist think tanks on both coasts. It is completely contrary to the foundational American principle that people and their rights are God-given, and that the government answers to the citizens, not the other way around.

"Equality" as the American ideal relates to our rights as a sovereign people who live freely under self-government. Now, it is true that the country didn't exactly live up to these ideals entirely throughout its history; but what's an ideal for, if not to give us something to strive to attain? America came into being having inherited the institution of slavery, and it took almost ninety years to settle that issue. And the legacy of slavery would continue, in some ways, up until the present day.

What most of us have been raised to believe is that equality means "equality of opportunity." This is the colorblind philosophy of the early Martin Luther King Jr., that people should "not be judged by the color of their skin but by the content of their character." This is a fairly inarguable sentiment, and one with which most Americans would agree.

People, especially children, should be given all credit for what they actually say and do, and our opinions of them should not be clouded by their race—be they black or white. So if a black youth does well on a competitive entrance exam, by all means he or she ought to be admitted to the school or hired for the job. Fair is fair.

We can note that this definition of equality is not exactly what Jefferson was talking about, but it's close enough, and seems like as good a way to organize a society as anything else. And the law requires it. Certainly, some people have rich parents, and some are born into poverty, but we try to offer all kids nutritious food and high-quality schools so they have the *equal opportunity* to succeed.

In the wake of King's assassination and the end of legalized discrimination in America, it seemed by the mid-seventies or so that we had achieved a kind of consensus on the meaning of equality. "Let's give everybody a fair shot." The Fourteenth Amendment to the Constitution, ratified in 1868, ensures the "equal protection of the laws" to everyone; the 1964 Civil Rights Act clarified the Fourteenth Amendment by specifically outlawing discrimination on the basis of race, color, sex, or national origin in voting requirements, in schools and public accommodations, and in hiring and other labor relations. America was on the road to equal opportunity.

But as the years ticked by, certain groups did better than others. Too many black Americans lagged behind. The Immigration and Nationality Act of 1965 abolished quotas for admission to the country, and over the next twenty years the complexion of America changed radically. It was no longer a question of a mostly white nation with a minority black population and a sprinkling of other races; America really did transform into a kind of racial hodgepodge.

The government kept track of each racial group—"Hispanics" were added to the census in 1970, and "Asian or Pacific Islander" was added in 1990—and their metrics in regard to social outcomes could be pored over and analyzed by brigades of sociologists and statisticians. Quotas, in the form of "affirmative action," were instituted to try to fine-tune the outcome disparities.

Different minority groups, rather than banding together in the pursuit of colorblind excellence through equality of opportunity, instead became increasingly race-conscious as they noted how much less they got of some resource, and how poorly their fared in some outcome.

Out of this obsessive attention to outcomes was born Critical Race Theory (CRT). CRT takes it as a given that the construction of race and ethnicity underwrites and affects most aspects of society. Even if we establish what appears to be an equal ground of opportunity for all, racism is built into our institutions to such a degree that it confounds our efforts to equalize conditions. Moreover, various forms of oppression work on different axes of identity, such that a black woman may face challenging conditions, even in an environment where blacks and women, as separate categories, may succeed.

CRT, a neo-Marxist concept, was an academic analytical theory in law schools for a few decades, but it slowly seeped into other university disciplines such as sociology and the humanities, and got a firm toehold in education schools, which train the nation's teachers. Soon a whole generation of professionals, teachers, professors, and even human resource personnel were versed in the idea that equality of opportunity was insufficient to deal with the problems that they saw in such a pervasively racist society as ours.

What emerged slowly and then all at once was a demand to ditch "equality" as a value and pursue "equity" instead. The best definition of equity was offered by Kamala Harris right before the 2020 election. Harris narrated a cartoon video that depicts two mountain climbers, one white and one black. The white climber begins his ascent from the base of the mountain, but the black climber begins in a deep hole.

"So there's a big difference between equality and equity," the future vice president begins. "Equality suggests, 'Oh, everyone should get the same amount.' The problem with that, not everybody's starting out at the same place."[1]

I don't know where Kamala Harris heard that equality means "everyone should get the same amount." Amount of what? But in any case, she concludes by explaining, "Equitable treatment means we all end up at the same place."

Disparate impact law already means that racial outcome disparities— say, in graduation rates—are evidence of discrimination. For example, in New York City, black applicants to become firefighters and teachers had higher than normal rates of failure on standardized tests, for decades. Recent court rulings and settlements have determined that the high failure rates are evidence that the tests were racist—they must have been racist, or the black applicants would have tested just as well as the white applicants. So now New York is paying over a billion dollars in back wages, medical benefits, and pension contributions to people who failed a test twenty or thirty years ago, compensating them as though they had been working firemen or teachers all along.

Saying "equitable treatment means we all end up at the same place" is a modern restatement of old-fashioned communism. It aims for "equality of outcome," whereas the accepted definition of equality since the sixties had been "equality of opportunity." The Left has substituted equity for equality. The two words sound similar, but the political implications behind these terms are radically different.

The embers had barely cooled on the George Floyd riots of 2020 when there suddenly emerged a demand for a national "racial reckoning." In addition to demands to defund police departments, remove the names and images of inconvenient historical figures from public spaces, and form commissions to assess how many trillions of dollars should be paid out in reparations for slavery, a new equity regime took hold across government, academia, and corporate head offices.

This new regime, born from the principles of Critical Race Theory, was called Diversity, Equity, and Inclusion (DEI) and quickly became the defining organizational purpose behind many American institutions. On his very first day as president in 2021, Joe Biden promised to "advance an ambitious, whole-of-government equity agenda."

The principle of equality of opportunity was old thinking that needed to be replaced, the Left argued. As the Biden White House explained, "although the ideal of equal opportunity is the bedrock of American democracy, our laws, public policies, and institutions too often exacerbate disparities or deny equal opportunity to individuals and communities."

The Order elaborated,

Entrenched disparities in our laws and public policies, and in our public and private institutions, have often denied that equal opportunity to individuals and communities. Our country faces converging economic, health, and climate crises that have exposed and exacerbated inequities, while a historic movement for justice has highlighted the unbearable human costs of systemic racism. Our Nation deserves an ambitious whole-of-government equity agenda that matches the scale of the opportunities and challenges that we face.

By advancing equity across the Federal Government, we can create opportunities for the improvement of communities that have been historically underserved, which benefits everyone. For example, an analysis shows that closing racial gaps in wages, housing credit, lending opportunities, and access to higher education would amount to an additional $5 trillion in gross domestic product in the American economy over the next 5 years. The Federal Government's goal in advancing equity is to provide everyone with the opportunity to reach their full potential.[2]

RIGHTS and FREEDOMS in PERIL

Note that the order refers explicitly to "public and private institutions." The equity regime is not just a whole-of-government program: its true remit is whole-of-society.

With staggering speed, human resources divisions—tagged now as "DEI Offices"—across the economy gained astonishing new authority, within corporations, on campuses, and throughout government. DEI officers assumed control over training, hiring, and participated in decision-making regarding business-critical matters at the highest levels. Overnight, "advancing equity" became not just a government slogan, but a national priority within every significant American institution—public and private.

This is no exaggeration. Major scientific research institutions now require all applicants to submit DEI statements detailing the extent of their commitment to the principles of inclusivity. It's not enough just to nod and agree with the sentiment; applicants to the Yale Department of Molecular Biophysics and Biochemistry are asked to specify ways in which they have "interacted with diverse groups," and to show a "sustained track-record of multiple efforts in promoting DEI." The UCLA medical school, which by state law is banned from using affirmative action in admissions, has nevertheless degraded its standards so much in its pursuit of admitting under-qualified racial minorities that half the students fail basic tests of medical competence.

The motto of Judicial Watch is "Because no one is above the law." It is our opinion that "Diversity, Equity, Inclusion," Critical Race Theory, and the equity agenda represent nothing less than a coup from within. The true constitutional model of ordered liberty, republican self-rule, and advancement on the basis of individual merit and hard work has been overturned in favor of an equalitarian, essentially communist ideal in which all social goods are distributed on the basis of racial caste.

In this intersectional race-based spoils system, points are awarded based on supposed lack of social prestige or privilege. According to this diabolical great chain of being, a white child from Appalachia who grew up impoverished nonetheless has more social status—more privilege—than the child of an upper-middle-class black professional in Manhattan. Part of the equity agenda is to turn the world upside down and ensure that society's goods are distributed according to the dictates of history. Of course, the real beneficiaries of this system are the apparatchiks—the equity officers in charge of assigning privilege points and deciding who gets to live where.

Simply put: Promoting "equity" requires tyranny. Promoting "equality" requires the rule of law and freedom.

Judicial Watch is committed to vindicating the rule of law and the US Constitution, which emerged from the essential American principle that rights flow from God to the people, who are the true sovereigns. We have filed multiple lawsuits to expose the chicanery of these race hustlers who hide their savage levelling instincts behind soft kindergarten words of fairness and sharing. As the civil rights organizations of the Left have retreated from promoting equality under law, Judicial Watch has become one of the foremost civil liberties organization in the United States. We devote ourselves continually to making sure that the American government, captured by the forces of social chaos and racialism, lives up to the promises of the Declaration's core truth that all men are created equated.

....

One of the first things the Biden administration set out to do was to make sure that the spirit of CRT pervaded the entire US government, especially in the military, where the established ideals of patriotism and honor still meant something. Less than a month after Biden's inauguration, Secretary of Defense Lloyd Austin ordered all departments of the military to conduct a one day "stand-down" to address supposed ideological extremism, i.e., conservatism, in the ranks.

"We will not tolerate actions that go against the fundamental principles of the oath we share, including actions associated with extremist or dissident ideologies," Secretary Austin advised in his memo to Pentagon leadership. "Service members, DoD civilian employees, and all those who support our mission, deserve an environment free of discrimination, hate, and harassment. It is incumbent upon each of us to ensure that actions associated with these corrosive behaviors are prevented."[3]

Well, that doesn't sound entirely unreasonable. Extremist ideologies aren't conducive to a military setting in which lines of command must be followed. Except Lloyd Austin and the designers of the stand-down weren't worried about all extremist ideologies; just the ones that violated the neo-Marxist tenets of the DEI regime promoted by the Biden administration.

Tommy Waller, a retired marine lieutenant colonel who was on duty at the time of the stand-down, notes that

> the materials issued to the force in relation to the "Extremism Stand-Down" deliberately omitted examples of U.S. Army soldiers conducting terrible acts of jihadist terrorism. Also missing were any examples of service members supporting Marxist BLM or Antifa violence. While I complied with the orders to conduct this "stand-down," to ensure that my Marines received balanced education covering all relevant threats, I included jihadist and left wing extremism—which they very much appreciated.
>
> Nor was my experience unique. Multiple service members complained that the "stand-down" training was ideologically slanted, and did not properly identify support for groups like Antifa or Black Lives Matter as inappropriate for active duty personnel.[4]

Waller notes that the case of Army Major Nidal Hasan, who killed thirteen soldiers and wounded thirty at Ford Hood, was not mentioned in the stand-down material. The radical anarchist beliefs that motivated Airman Aaron Bushnell to burn himself to death in front of the Israeli Embassy and inspired Bradley/Chelsea Manning to commit espionage were of no interest to the stand-down architects, either.

At Judicial Watch we recalled Lloyd Austin's testimony at his confirmation hearing, held less two weeks after the January 6 riot, where he explicitly connected the supposed extremism of the Capitol protestors to the "racists and extremists" in the military. "The job of the Department of Defense is to keep America safe from our enemies. But we can't do that if some of those enemies lie within our own ranks," Austin told the Senate Armed Services Committee.

Judicial Watch asked the Department of Defense to turn over all emails from top Pentagon brass related to the Countering Extremism Working Group that Secretary Austin established in April 2021. When they refused our request, we were forced to sue. "Why is the Pentagon's leadership hiding records about its ongoing political purge and attack on the First Amendment rights of our troops?" I asked at the time.

The partisan nature of the hunt for "extremism" in the military was confirmed by the selection of Bishop Garrison, Senior Advisor to the Secretary of Defense on Human Capital and Diversity, Equity, and Inclusion, to head up the CEWG. In July 2019, Garrison tweeted of then-president Donald Trump:

Silence from our Congressional leaders is complicity. He is only going to get worse from here, & his party and its leadership are watching it happen while doing nothing to stop it. Support for him, a racist, is support for ALL his beliefs.

He's dragging a lot of bad actors (misogynist, extremists, other racists) out into the light, normalizing their actions. If you support the President, you support that. There is no room for nuance with this. There is no more "but I'm not like that" talk.[5]

A month later, Garrison wrote, "now, arguably more than at any time in recent history, we need to recognize that extremism, racist policies, and white supremacy stand as existential threats not only to American life but to the future of our country and others around the globe." He went on to prescribe the *New York Times*'s tendentious "1619 Project" as an antidote to the supposed "nation-ending threat of white supremacy and white nationalist extremism."

The "1619 Project," assembled by non-historian Nikole Hannah-Jones, purports to explain that the true founding of the United States should be dated to 1619, when the first shipment of African slaves landed in Virginia. Hannah-Jones argues that slavery and anti-black racism were the inspiration and foundation for the formation of America, and that all American history is shot through with anti-black racism. Even the Thirteenth Amendment, which freed the slaves, is just a clever means of re-enslaving black people, through a clause specifying that involuntary servitude can be demanded "as punishment for crime whereof the party shall have been duly convicted."

This noxious tome, which was roundly debunked by scholars across the political spectrum, became a basic text of the Critical Race Theory agenda, and explains for all to see the perspective of the "woke," or racialized communist, Left. America, according to CRT ideology, is essentially a revolting wasteland of racial violence and white denial. And this was a favorite book of the head of the "Countering Extremism Working Group" in Biden's Pentagon!

But the perversion of military training didn't start with the "Stand-Down" or the formation of the CEWG. In July 2020, Judicial Watch obtained 1,483 pages of teaching materials and twenty-six pages of budget records from the Department of Defense produced by the Defense Equal Opportunity Management Institute (DEOMI) that are used by "equal opportunity advisors" to train service members on diversity topics. The documents were obtained in response to a Judicial Watch FOIA request.

The teaching materials include "Student Study Guides" written for "Equal Opportunity Advisor Courses" that are critical of persons who "believe that human similarities are more important than differences"; advise people to acknowledge their privilege when "it is pointed out to them"; claim that heterosexuals have "sexual orientation privilege"; and that "religious privilege" exists.

According to DEOMI's website, the organization was "Propelled by the civil rights movement of the 1960s." The DEOMI operating budget between 2012 and 2017 totaled $19.66 million. According to the Defense Department Comptroller's office, DEOMI and WRP (Workforce Recruitment Program) jointly make up an entity called the Defense Management Operations Center (DMOC) and that entity was budgeted $13,366,000 for the 2020 fiscal year.[6]

The records included a chapter called "Power and Privilege," in which students are taught that "Privilege can also be linked to various forms of identity such as . . . sexual orientation privilege" and "religious privilege." Students were also taught that there is "sexual orientation privilege" associated with the "marginalization of non-heterosexual lifestyles and the view that heterosexuality is the normal sexual orientation."

In a key and telling passage, the guide advised that "some dominant group members" may claim "personal achievement mostly depends on personal ability." This contention, that merit and hard work are just a screen for unearned placement at the top of society, is truly at the core of the equity agenda. How disgusting that our military, our oldest and proudest institution, should be instructed in these filthy, communist lies.

The study guide also taught that people who raise religious objections to homosexual marriage are engaged in a form of discrimination called "principium," which is "avoiding exploration based on a religious or personal principle. A person using this philosophy might state, 'I find it upsetting and disheartening that homosexuals, or anyone for that matter, would have to bear such injustices. However, I do not believe that it is an injustice or discriminatory act to not allow homosexuals couples to cross the threshold of qualifications to be married.'"

It's not clear what sort of "exploration" the authors of this document expect religious people to undertake to make them reject the principles of their faith. But in order to "become personally aware of privilege," the study guide advised people to "decode your social identity."

In a chapter on diversity, the guide is critical of those who engage in "minimization," which it defines as those who believe that "human similarities are more important than differences." So much for the MLK doctrine that difference is only skin deep, or the foundational premise that we are all equal in God's eyes.

The guide notes that "Statistics show Whites [*sic*] are the majority in senior leadership positions (i.e., flag officers, general officers, and Senior Executive Service) and lend itself [*sic*] to the perpetuation of racism." (The Left's new insistence on the capitalization of racial terms such as "Black" and "White" is pernicious racialism that would be at home in apartheid-era South Africa.)

An example of "modern racism" is saying things like "Discrimination is a thing of the past . . . tactics and demands of activists are unfair . . . racism is bad." The document also states that another form of racism is "aversive racism." Aversive racists, say the authors, "put high value on egalitarian beliefs."

In a chart labeled "Racist Behavior" the authors break racism into "traditional," "symbolic," "modern," and "aversive" categories, in which modern racists believe minorities are "undeserving of special efforts to redress past inequities." The chart also indicates that people who oppose "policies designed to address racial equality" or feel that those policies are violations of "norms and fairness" are modern racists.

Students are encouraged to: "Talk to others about your recognized inferior socialized behavior." In a learning bloc on "Perceptions" equal opportunity advisors are told that "stereotypes are bad if they lead to discrimination of protected categories." After cautioning against using stereotypes in previous study sections, the study section on Asian Americans says, "Self-control, discipline, competitiveness, and education are important elements in Japanese American culture." So some stereotypes are okay, it seems.

Tellingly, a warning footer at the bottom of the trainer's guides, repeated throughout the document advises "FOR TRAINING PURPOSES ONLY—DO NOT USE ON THE JOB." [Emphasis in original.]

A section addressing "Cross-Cultural Communication" states: "Gender includes the social construction of masculinity and femininity within a culture and incorporates his or her biological, psychological, and sociological characteristics. Sex refers to a person's biological or physical self. Although sex determines who will bear children, gender accounts for our roles in life and how these life roles affect our communication."

The section also claims that in childhood gender communication: "Girls are told to use their manners, play quietly, and be ladylike," it is "okay for boys to use rough language, play loudly, and be rambunctious. Girls are allowed to show feelings."

After warning readers about the dangers of stereotypes, the manual then says women communicate "stereotypically . . . using a passive/assertive style," whereas men communicate "stereotypically" by "using an assertive/aggressive style in efforts to accomplish tasks, achieve status, and dominate the conversation."

A section on "Sexual Orientation Privilege" includes the view that this group believes "heterosexuality is the normal sexual orientation," and that "sexual and marital relations are normal only when between people of different sexes." The guide notes that transsexual, transgender, and sometimes homosexual populations are denied "freedom enjoyed by heterosexual couples."

The guide advises Equal Opportunity Advisors to: "Acknowledge your privilege when it is pointed out to you." They are also told that "Privilege will never go away until the systems in our society that cause discrimination go away," and suggests that the equal opportunity advisors "work to make those inequitable systems visible."

In a fifteen-page study guide on "Extremism," the guide mentions Nazis, white supremacism, criminal gangs, skinhead groups, the Confederate flag, national anarchists, eco-terrorism, environmental activists, and right-wing extremists. Three pages discuss "skinhead culture."

In a discussion of the history of sexism in the military, the guide claims that "many women masqueraded as men in order to serve their country." While there are a few such cases in American military history, the rare examples hardly seem worth citing as a statement on the malleability of traditional sex roles.

In a study guide on "Diversity Management," the authors advise that affirmative action "focuses on prevention and/or correcting discriminatory practices concerned with numbers of minorities and women. It is an attempt to rectify past discrimination against certain groups of people." In the next paragraph, the authors write: "Service members shall be evaluated only on merit, fitness, and capability. Unlawful discrimination against individuals or groups based on race, color, religion, sex, or national origin is contrary to good order and discipline and . . . shall not be condoned."

The documents contain bizarre, innumerate statements. In a study guide section on "White Americans," the authors say that "The majority, 35.7 percent, of White Americans are located in the South (US Census Bureau, 2010)." In a study guide section on Hispanic Americans, the authors describe illegal aliens from Mexico as "undocumented Mexican immigrants."

"These documents show that the Department of Defense has been indoctrinating our troops with anti-American and racially inflammatory 'training,'" I said at the time. "We must protect our military service members from being brainwashed by the divisive, anti-American propaganda fueling the leftist insurrectionists who are right now trying to destroy our country."[7]

The indoctrination of our service personnel worsened under the Biden administration. In November 2022, Judicial Watch again sued the Department of Defense to obtain US Air Force Academy training materials related to Critical Race Theory. The records include a PowerPoint presentation titled "Political Psychology, Lessons 32–33: Prejudice and Racism." On a slide labeled "Race and Partisanship" is a bullet stating, "Opposition to interracial dating correlated with white partisanship after Obama's election despite being unrelated to party identification in previous decades."

The presentation includes a set of tables with the headline "White Americans' Support for Democratic Candidates for President as a Function of Old-Fashioned Racism." Another slide depicts tables that purport to show "Correlations between Republican Party Identification and Old-Fashioned Racism among White Americans."

A slide titled "Racialization of Public Policy" includes a bullet stating, "They [pollsters] found that the image of a black man greatly impacted responses among Trump supporters." The next bullet asserts:

After being exposed to the black racial cue, Trump voters:

- Were less supportive of housing assistance programs
- Expressed higher levels of anger that some people receive government assistance

- Were more likely to say that individuals who receive assistance are to blame for their economic situation.

Another slide purports to show a chart depicting "White Identity among White Americans," with the subtitle "How Important Is Being White to Your Identity?" Additional slides are titled "How White Identity Shapes Politics" and contain tables purporting to show:

- Effect of White Identity on Empathy toward People of Color
- Effect of White Identity on Support for Voter ID Laws
- Effect of White Identity on Support for Political Violence

A slide titled "Race and Politics" includes an image of President Obama with the bullet "Because the President is the leader of his respective party—Obama signified a massive shift in image of the stereotypical Democrat," followed by the bullet: "The Democratic party became branded as the party of Black Americans."

This overtly partisan signaling explicitly informed future leaders of the Air Force that the Republican Party is racist, pro-white, and seeks to harm black Americans.

A "CRT Talking Points" document prepared at the direction of the Air Force Academy Superintendent includes the question "Does CRT teach cadets to hate our country?" The scripted "academic answer" to the question asserts, "much of what is 'divisive' [about CRT] is that it's hard for people to hear the words 'white supremacy' without feeling defensive, even though that is the academically correct way to talk about most of American history."

The records include a transcript of Defense Secretary Lloyd Austin's June 23, 2021, congressional testimony in which he tells Representative Matt Gaetz, "I don't know what the issue of critical race theory is and what the relevance here in the department. We do not teach critical race theory. We don't embrace critical race theory. And I think that's a spurious conversation."

This is a common stratagem regarding discussion of CRT by its advocates. Proponents dishonestly dismiss questions or criticism about the prevalence of CRT by insisting that it's an obscure legal theory that only comes up in third-year law school classes or graduate-level political philosophy seminars.[8]

Indeed, just two weeks after Austin's "we don't teach CRT" testimony, on July 7, 2021, Air Force Academy Dean of Faculty Brigadier General Linell Letendre forwards to Superintendent Lieutenant General Richard Clark, Commander of Cadets Brigadier General Paul Moga, and others whose names are redacted, a *Washington Post* opinion piece written the previous day by USAFA Professor Lynne Chandler Garcia, titled "Why U.S. military academies should teach critical race theory." Letendre adds a note promoting the piece:

> My thanks to Dr. Chandler Garcia for putting into words what many of us have expressed to each other around the water coolers about the importance of teaching our cadets *how to think*. [Emphasis in original.] As future leaders of the profession of arms, we owe them nothing less.

An August 13, 2021, email exchange between academy officials details hosting a virtual discussion with Stephen Brookfield, author of *Teaching Race: How to Help Students Unmask and Challenge Racism*, to USAFA faculty members. One official raises concerns over Brookfield's discussion topics related to Critical Race Theory.

In a separate email chain, a person whose name is redacted sends the Brookfield event information to Letendre: "In case this slipped your notice, I just wanted to make sure you and the dean were aware that the [redacted] book group initiative has the potential to further the CRT storm." The dean replies, "Thanks for the SA [situational awareness]. No concerns. We need to keep doing the right things to prepare and develop faculty." Forty-three faculty members signed up for Brookfield's talk.

Another presentation discusses the teachings of Brookfield and has the headline "The (White) Elephant in the Room" and bullets that are partially obscured.

A slide in the series has the title "Team Teaching" and includes the bullet: "Allows you to . . . Demonstrate how to engage in difficult conversations in a way focused on behaviors not personhood, & on learned white supremacy not essential moral differences or failings." Another bullet states: "Allows you to . . . Facilitate racial affinity groups."

Another slide is titled "The Fatigue of WWW—Witnessing White Woke-ness." An additional slide proposes:

A calculus of understanding amongst Black, Indigenous and People of Color (BIPOC) who have negotiated the dynamics of structural racism all their lives & are tired of *WITNESSING "WOKENESS"* in White people coming to new racial awareness. [Emphasis in original.]

One of the Brookfield slides is titled "Hard Truths I've Learned as a White Instructor/Leader" and contains bullets such as "I MUST assume that for students and colleagues of color, EVERYTHING is seen through the lens of race. For them, NOTHING is 'race free.'" And "I MUST acknowledge my own racist behavior when it's pointed out to me—not to try to 'explain' it away, not protest my innocence." [Emphases in original.]

Still another Brookfield slide contains the bullets "I MUST NEVER ask people of color to teach me about racism—figuring out what whites should do is MY responsibility" and "I MUST NEVER 'confess' my racism so as to seek 'absolution' from BIPOC students & colleagues." [Emphasis in original.]

Perhaps the most pernicious aspect of this ideological indoctrination is the idea that white people are necessarily guilty of racism, and this guilt is historical. Regardless of the personal, or even familial, history of the individual, they carry a presumption of guilt and are assumed to owe a massive, unresolved debt to non-whites. In communist nations, class status is imputed to people based on who their parents or grandparents were. In today's version of racialized communism, status is strictly a matter of race.

Among the works written by Brookfield listed in the bibliography is "Creating an Anti-Racist White Identity." A presentation, which has no specification as to whether it is intended for faculty or the students, is titled "Free Speech in the Military" and has a slide labeled "The Commie Cadet," which includes images of West Point cadet Spencer Rapone at his graduation ceremony showing the inside of his cap in which is written "Communism will win," and one of him wearing a Che Guevara T-shirt under his uniform.

A presentation, apparently intended for the cadets, is titled "American Political System & Theory, Lesson 25–31 Law & Democracy," and a slide containing a list of information under "Things to Know," which describes Critical Race Theory as: "Critical Race Theory studies racism as a social construct" and "Proponents say learning the history of racism is crucial to addressing inequities."

Lesson 14 of a Social Sciences presentation is titled "What does Race have to do with Security?" The next slide, titled "Critical Race Theory," provides several bullet points of "definitions" of CRT, such as: "A collection of critical stances against the existing legal order from a race-based point of view (Brooks 1994)."

The view that the law and legal institutions are inherently racist and that race itself, instead of being biologically grounded and natural, is a socially constructed concept that is used by white people to further their economic and political interests at the expense of people of color. (Curry 2009)

Another slide discusses the "'Myth' of American Peoplehood" with one bullet claiming: "The U.S. too has a creation myth: The Declaration of Independence declares that all men have rights endowed by their Creator; Ideas of social contracts forged in a state of nature."

In the same Social Sciences presentation is a slide titled: "Lesson 16: Black Lives Matter—Causes and Context." A bloc of slides in the presentation discusses BLM, with one slide alleging: "White privilege doesn't mean your life hasn't been **hard**. It means that your skin color isn't one of the things making it **harder**." [Emphasis in original.]

Various slides promoting BLM follow, including one depicting a white police officer holding a sign pointing to a black man, asking, "Is his life worth less than mine?" and a white woman holding a similar sign pointing to a black woman.

Numerous slides depict alleged police brutality against blacks, one of which states, "Nearly 90% of documented force used by FPD [the Ferguson, Missouri Police Department] was used against African Americans." Ferguson is about 75 percent black, and given high rates of crime among the local community, it is not altogether shocking that most use of force by the police are against black residents.

"The Air Force is fomenting racialism, racial separatism and segregation, and anti-white hatred among its rising young leadership at the Air Force Academy," I noted. "These documents show the Biden Defense Department is teaching these cadets on how to hate America using repackaged revolutionary Marxist propaganda."

Reviewing all this material leads one to the disturbing conclusion that the Left indoctrinators running the Biden administration seek to alienate our military from the America they are expected to defend and protect. A military brainwashed to advance the anti-American Marxism is a extremist Left dream, and a patriotic American's nightmare.[9]

. . . .

The malevolent influence of CRT is by no means limited to the US military. Judicial Watch uncovered CRT lesson plans being implemented in school districts around the country. In May 2021, we received 685 pages of heavily redacted records from Montgomery County Maryland Public Schools, including documents related to their "Anti-racist system audit" and Critical Race Theory classes

The documents, obtained under the Maryland Public Information Act, reveal that students of "Maryland's Largest School District" who attended Thomas Pyle Middle School's social justice class were taught that the phrase "Make America Great Again" was an example of "covert white supremacy." The phrase is ranked on a pyramid just below "lynching," "hate crimes," "the N-word," and "racial slurs." They were also taught that "white privilege" means being favored by school authorities and having a positive relationship with the police.

Additionally, the documents show that Montgomery County Public Schools allocated over $454,000 for an "Anti-racist system audit" by the Mid-Atlantic Equity Consortium, a company that claims that their "expertise in using intersectionality as part of its theory of change makes us uniquely positioned to conduct the Anti-Racist Audit and mitigate the root causes of systemic barriers."

In Thomas Pyle Middle School's "social justice" class course curriculum, there is a slide titled "What is systemic racism?" in which students are shown a pyramid slide depicting "Differences between overt and covert hateful white supremacy." According to the pyramid,

"Make America Great Again" is an example of "covert white supremacy." The phrase is ranked on a pyramid just below "racial slurs."

Examples of other covert "white supremacy" include thinking "but we're just one human family," "colorblindness," "cultural appropriation," "celebration of Columbus Day," "police murdering POC [people of color]," and "bootstrap theory." A separate pyramid begins with the term "genocide."

The documents include Mid-Atlantic Equity Consortium's "anti-racist system audit" proposal, which describes intersectional theory as "people are often disadvantaged by multiple sources of oppression: their race, class, gender identity, native language, sexual orientation, religion, and other identity markers. Intersectionality recognizes that identity markers (e.g. "female" and "Black") do not exist independently of each other, and that each informs the others, often creating a complex merging of oppression."

Records regarding Montgomery County Public School's Thomas W. Pyle Middle School's social justice class include a cover letter, noting that the class in question was a one-week "Summer Boost" class called "Reading and Taking Action for Social Justice" offered from July 13–17, 2020, and that "no grades were given and no actual work due." The class material includes a push for students to fill out a form letter with contact information addressed to federal, state, and county education officials asking for more Critical Race Theory classes in schools.

In a slide titled "What is Intersectionality?" the students are told it is defined as:

Exposing [one's] multiple identities can help clarify the ways in which a person can simultaneously experience privilege and oppression. . . .

Per [Critical Race Theory scholar] Kimberlé Williams Crenshaw, "Intersectionality is simply a prism to see the

Interactive effects of various forms of discrimination and disempowerment. It looks at the way that racism, many times, interacts with patriarchy, heterosexism, classism, xenophobia—seeing that the overlapping vulnerabilities created by these systems actually create specific kinds of challenges."

A class slide titled "Implicit Bias, Structural Racism" states:

Race is created to justify enslaving people from Africa (economic engine of country).

National narrative (ideology, belief system) about people of color being "less than" human (and less than white) justifies mistreatment and inequality (white supremacy).

Dominant narratives about race (family, media, society) coupled with racialized structural arrangements and differential outcomes by race all prime us to believe that people of color are inferior to white people . . .

The students are asked: "What is White Privilege?" and are instructed that white privilege includes, among other things: having "a positive relationship with the police, generally"; "soaking in media blatantly biased toward my race"; and "living ignorant of the dire state of racism today."

The students are suggested to view a Ted Talk interview with Patrisse Cullors, a founder of Black Lives Matter. The class is provided "definitions" created by www.racialequitytools.org. The terms that are defined include:

- "Black Lives Matter," which is defined as "A political movement to address systemic and state violence against African Americans." It claims that "Black Lives Matter is an ideological and political intervention in a world where Black lives are systematically and intentionally targeted for demise."

- "Power," defined among other things as: "Wealth, whiteness, citizenship, patriarchy, heterosexism, and education are a few key social mechanisms through which power operates."
- "Racist policies" is defined with the statement "There is no such thing as a nonracist or race-neutral policy."
- "White Privilege," which is defined as "to the unquestioned and unearned set of advantages, entitlements, benefits, and choices bestowed on people solely because they are white." And "Structure white privilege" is described as "A system of white domination that creates and maintains belief systems that make current racial advantages and disadvantages seem normal."
- Under the heading "White Supremacy," "White supremacy culture" is defined as referring, "to the dominant, unquestioned standards of behavior and ways of functioning embodied by the vast majority of institutions in the United States." White supremacy culture is further defined as "the glue that binds together white-controlled institutions into systems and white-controlled systems into the global white supremacy system."
- Other defined terms include: "Anti-black," "colonization," "racial recognition," "racialization," "structural racism," and "whiteness"

Judicial Watch also received records relating to Montgomery County Public School's Greenwood Elementary School's "Dual Pandemic" of "Covid-19/systemic racism" class presentation.[10]

"The racist, revolutionary claptrap in these documents should be nowhere near a school classroom," I said at the time. "These documents show that extremists have access to our schools and are willing to abuse this access to children in order to advance a dangerous, divisive, and likely illegal agenda."[11]

Later in 2021, a Rhode Island whistleblower gave Judicial Watch access to a training document from the Westerly School District showing how Westerly Public Schools are using teachers to push Critical Race Theory in classrooms.

The training course was assembled by the left-leaning Highlander Institute and cites quotes from Bettina Love, from whom the Biden administration distanced itself publicly after she made statements equating "whiteness" to oppression.

The school district continues to deny that it teaches Critical Race Theory. This is the same ruse I described above, where school districts simultaneously claim that they don't know what CRT is, have never heard of it, and certainly don't teach it, while in reality they structure entire curricula around the equalitarian principles of CRT.

But the document reveals the following anti-American communism:

- The training course claims that there are "unfortunate truths" about the history of Rhode Island and the United States."
- The training course notes that there is "systemic inequity" that must be overcome in the school system.
- The training course asks teachers, "How does systemic racism manifest itself in the education experience for students?"
- The training course links to a video called "Systemic Racism Explained" from Act.TV, a far-left YouTube channel.
- The course instructs teachers to ask themselves, "How do I challenge systemic inequity as an educator?"
- The course goals are to "foster and sustain cultural pluralism, ultimately for the purpose of social transformation." Further, its stated goal is to "disrupt the impact of educational inequity and empower students to transform their own lives, their communities, and society."

The course highlights "A Framework for Culturally Responsive & Sustaining Pedagogy," which includes:

- "Awareness" that "we all operate within an inequitable system"
- "Cognitive Development" where teachers "leverage students' identities and interests . . ." and "scaffold and develop students' thinking skills"
- "Critical Consciousness" where the goal is that students are motivated to "critical action so they can transform their lives, communities, and society."
- The course teaches that teachers should focus on collectivism over individualism.
- In order to promote collectivism, it states that teachers may have to "gather information about students' identities . . . " in order to have them reflect. These activities link to a journaling activity where students are prompted to write about the demographics of their neighborhood.

"This whistleblower document shows yet another school district, under the rubric of critical race theory, that wants to use teachers to abuse their positions to turn children into Marxist agitators," I noted. "Rather than threatening parents, the Justice Department should be investigating this rampant racism being pushed by leftist extremists in schools across America."[12]

The CRT/DEI political regime doesn't limit itself to trying to fix entities under its direct control, like schools and the military, however. Its impact is broad and infects every major American institution.

The United States system of justice is supposed to be blind to race, sex, and status. The law is, famously, "no respecter of persons." So when federal judges issued orders that gave special preference to attorneys who appear before them based on the lawyers' race, ethnicity, or gender/sex, Judicial Watch immediately filed a judicial misconduct complaint.

The complaint named Chief Judge Nancy J. Rosenstengel, Judge Staci M. Yandle, and Judge David W. Dugan for orders Judicial Watch states are discriminatory and unconstitutional and constitute "conduct prejudicial to the effective and expeditious administration of the business of the courts."

On January 7, 2020, Judge Yandle entered a standing order that provides:

> Recognizing the importance of the development of future generations of practitioners through courtroom opportunities, the undersigned encourages the participation of newer, female, and minority attorneys in proceedings in my courtroom, particularly with respect to oral argument . . . To that end, the Court adopts the following procedures regarding oral arguments as to pending motions:

> 1. After a motion is fully briefed, as part of a Motion Requesting Oral Argument, a party may alert the Court that, if oral argument is granted, it intends to have a newer, female, or minority attorney argue the motion (or a portion of the motion).
> 2. If such a request is made, the Court will:
> A. Grant the request for oral argument on the motion it if is at all practicable to do so.
> B. Strongly consider allocating additional time for oral argument beyond what the Court may otherwise have allocated were a newer, female, or minority attorney not arguing the motion.

C. Permit other more experienced counsel of record the ability to provide some assistance to the newer, female, or minority attorney who is arguing the motion, where appropriate during oral argument.

Chief Judge Rosenstengel entered a nearly identical standing order on January 17, 2020, followed by Judge David W. Dugan doing the same on October 6, 2020.

These orders are patently discriminatory and unconstitutional, as well as patronizing and deeply offensive. They also plainly imply that female and minority attorneys are less competent, less skilled, and less qualified than male and non-minority attorneys and require additional time and assistance to represent their clients.

Moreover, they send a clear message to clients that, if they hire female or minority attorneys, they will be afforded advantages that they will not be afforded if they hire male or non-minority attorneys. They also erode litigants' and the public's trust and confidence in the justice system.

Courtroom time is a finite resource, and allowing oral argument, additional time, or the assistance of additional counsel based on immutable characteristics like race, ethnicity, and sex/gender is the antithesis of justice and fairness.

"This woke discrimination has no place in America's courtrooms," I said at the time. "It is frankly shocking that any federal judge would think it appropriate to engage in flagrant race and sex discrimination in this day and age."[13]

The good news is that these orders were rescinded!

The Judicial Council of the Seventh Circuit, which considered our complaint, issued a ruling that vindicated our concerns. The ruling notes:

In sum, all three judges have rescinded the standing orders that are the subject of these complaints. They also revised their case-management procedures, which now state only that the judges "welcome" or "encourage" oral argument by "relatively inexperienced attorneys." The judges no longer have a policy of preferential treatment for new or inexperienced attorneys or any other particular group of lawyers; more specifically, the judges have eliminated their prior policies of preferential treatment based on a lawyer's sex, gender, race, or ethnicity.

The Judicial Council also released letters from each of the three judges.

Chief US District Judge Nancy J. Rosenstengel acknowledged she "chose the wrong means to accomplish my goal of expanding courtroom opportunities for young lawyers. As worded, the Standing Order created perceived preferences based on immutable characteristics. As such, my procedures have been revised, and the Standing Order eliminated." (Judge Rosenstengel denied having made any decisions on the basis of any immutable characteristic.)

US District Judge Staci M. Yandle wrote: "While I have never granted or denied oral argument to an attorney based on their sex or race, nor would I, I acknowledge that as worded, the procedure and Standing Order created a perception of preferences based on immutable characteristics."

A third judge, US District Court Judge David W. Dugan, noted he had actually changed the order at issue in 2022 and that he had "not on any occasion in my now seven years on both the State and Federal benches granted, denied or even seriously entertained access to oral argument specifically or to our court generally on the basis of race, sex, age, or any immutable characteristic, nor will I in the future. Still, I recognize and acknowledge how such references could cause confusion for someone and, for that, I am regretful."

This was a remarkable victory for judicial ethics, accountability, and transparency. The courts did the right thing in acknowledging and correcting their mistakes in a public way.

We can hope that this quick and decisive result sends a signal to any other courts to end any "woke" policies that perpetuate discrimination and undermine confidence in the fair administration of justice.

A set of cases Judicial Watch brought against the state of California for aggrieved taxpayers gives me the most personal satisfaction of our many victories. In 2018 and 2019, California passed a couple of laws that mandated public corporations registered in the state—which includes some of the biggest companies in the world—to engage in race, sex, and other illicit discrimination.

The first law, known as Senate Bill 826, required publicly held corporations headquartered in California to have at least one director "who self-identifies her gender as a woman" on their boards by December 31, 2019 (Robin Crest et al. v. Alex Padilla [No.19ST-CV-27561]). Up to three such persons would be required by December 31, 2021, depending on the size of the board.

The second bill, Assembly Bill 979, required the same corporations to have a minimum of one director from an "underrepresented community" on its board by the end of the 2021 calendar year, and up to three "underrepresented-community" board members by the end of the 2022 calendar year, depending on the size of the board. The bill defines "director from an underrepresented community" to mean "an individual who self-identifies as Black, African American, Hispanic, Latino, Asian, Pacific Islander, Native American, Native Hawaiian, or Alaska Native, or who self-identifies as gay, lesbian, bisexual, or transgender."[14]

Now, to be honest, a lot of big California companies are pretty woke already, and corporations like Apple or Google probably go out of their way to keep their boards "diverse" as it is. But we didn't bring suit out of concern for what massive Big Tech companies do or don't do with their board composition. We brought suit because these laws brazenly violated anti-discrimination laws, with white, heterosexual males as the explicitly targeted victims.

First of all, a board of directors is supposed to oversee the operation of a company on behalf of its shareholders.

Forcing corporate boards to follow a race-/sex-based quota scheme is manifestly illegal.

You may have heard that California extremist legislation typically makes its way across the country—that what starts in California, doesn't stay in California. Allowed to stand, these quota mandates would have set a pattern for the rest of America, enforcing a system of racial and gender preferences for the appointment of corporate boards. And that would have been a first step toward imposing quotas throughout the rest of the economy as well.

California argued that that quotas not only remedy discrimination but also improve overall corporate performance. But our expert analysis debunked this myth as it related to the gender quota mandate: "The evidence offered for each of these points (underrepresentation of women on boards, discrimination as the cause of this underrepresentation, and that research shows a differential benefit of appointing women, as opposed to men, in terms of firm performance) is deficient and unreliable."[15]

For the purposes of corporate governance, it may be true that diversity is helpful. But by that we mean diversity of *expertise*. It would be good to have some directors who are experts in corporate finance, and others in corporate law or labor management. Having people who understand the core business and industry would be helpful, and it might be good to have directors who understand the communities in which the business operates.

That is totally separate from the question of the immutable characteristics of the members of the board of directors. If the best people to sit on the board are all black and Latino women, fine. If they are white men, same answer. The point is to find the best people, period.

Regarding the gender quota law, Judicial Watch argued, "SB 826 is illegal under the California Constitution. The legislation's quota system for female representation on corporate boards employs express gender classifications. As a result, SB 826 is immediately suspect and presumptively invalid and triggers strict scrutiny review."

The courts agreed with Judicial Watch, and struck down both laws. In April 2022, the California Superior Court released its full opinion in the case declaring that the state's racial, ethnic, and LGBT quota for diversity on corporate boards of California-based corporations violates the California Constitution. The court found that only in "very particular cases should discrimination be remedied by more discrimination."

Judge Terry A. Green found the law "violates the Equal Protection Clause of the California Constitution on its face." The judge elaborated why the California Legislature exceeded its authority in mandating the composition of boards:

> The difficulty is that the Legislature is thinking in group terms. But the California Constitution protects the right of *individuals* to equal treatment. Before the Legislature may require that members of one group be given certain board seats, it must first try to create neutral conditions under which qualified individuals from *any* group may succeed. That attempt was not made in this case. [Emphasis in original.]

The court concluded:

> The statute treats similarly situated individuals—qualified potential corporate board members—differently based on their membership (or lack thereof) in certain listed racial, sexual orientation, and gender identity groups. It requires that a

certain specific number of board seats be reserved for members of the groups on the list—and necessarily excludes members of other groups from those seats.

The secretary has not identified a compelling interest to justify this classification. The broader public benefits produced by well-run businesses do not fit that bill.

This was exactly the legal outcome we had hoped for. A month later, ruling on the gender equity case, California Superior Court Judge Maureen Duffy-Lewis, after a lengthy trial, agreed with Judicial Watch's lawyers and "determine[d] that SB 826 violates the Equal Protection Clause of the California Constitution and is thus enjoined."

In the court's twenty-three-page verdict, the court specifically found that "S.B. 826's goal was to achieve general equity or parity; its goal was not to boost California's economy, not to improve opportunities for women in the workplace nor not to protect California taxpayers, public employees, pensions and retirees."[16]

Further, the court found that "putting more women on boards demonstrated that the Legislature's actual purpose was gender-balancing, not remedying discrimination."

"There is no Compelling Governmental interest in remedying discrimination in the board selection process because neither the Legislature nor Defendant could identify any specific, purposeful, intentional and unlawful discrimination to be remedied," Judge Duffy-Lewis said.

The courts eviscerated California's unconstitutional quota mandates as unconstitutional. The radical Left's unprecedented attacks on anti-discrimination law suffered another stinging defeats thanks to Judicial Watch.

How pleasing it is to see California courts, which have a reputation for liberal activism, upholding the core American value of equal protection under the law.

Our taxpayer clients are heroes for standing up for civil rights against the Left's pernicious efforts to undo anti-discrimination protections.

Our legal team has helped protect the civil rights of every American with these successful lawsuits.

California, though, needs constant monitoring on its woke discrimination. San Francisco, unsurprisingly, took it to the next level with a race-based program to help black and Latino males who thought themselves transgender. So no whites, no Asians, etc. of any sex could benefit and, incredibly, no black females were eligible.

The program of course allowed illegal aliens to apply; allowed people who "engage in survival sex trades" to apply; and the use of the funds by participants was virtually unrestricted.

The city's mayoral office detailed how the program would "provide low-income transgender San Franciscans with $1,200 each month, up to 18 months to help address financial insecurity within trans communities."

Again, Judicial Watch stepped up against the lawlessness and filed a taxpayer lawsuit to stop the madness:

Applicants who do not identify as transgender, non-binary, gender non-conforming, or intersex are not eligible to participate in the GIFT program.

Applicants are prioritized based on their biological sex and race/ethnicity. Biological males identifying as female are given preference over biological females identifying as male, and applicants identifying as Black or Latino are given preference over applicants identifying as other races/ethnicities.[17]

This is in-your-face race and sex discrimination. As this book goes to press, we just heard from San Francisco's lawyer that the program is ending and won't be restarted. The Left pushes and Judicial Watch pushes back under law, and the Left retreats.

In 2021 the City of Asheville, North Carolina, instituted a brazen woke discriminatory program for scholarships to be "awarded in perpetuity to black high school students within Asheville City Schools, with special consideration given for black students pursuing a career in education."

We then filed a civil rights lawsuit in federal court on behalf of a citizens group whose members included high school students who were not eligible for these scholarships based solely on their race.

Our clients settled the lawsuit after Asheville quickly dropped these egregious race requirements.

Asheville's City Council approved a resolution that removes the racial criteria for the scholarship:

[T]he scholarship will give preference to applicants whose household members, including parents and/or guardians who have a high school education or less, these applicants representing "first generation" college students.

The City Council also removed racially discriminatory language for a scholarship program for educators and staff of Asheville City Schools.

The scholarship agreements were also amended to prohibit discrimination based on race and other categories.

This federal lawsuit and the resulting remarkable settlement should serve as a wake-up call to those activists and allied politicians pushing the extremist leftist agenda to segregate and discriminate based on race.

But the Left hasn't given up ignoring and trying to blow up the constitutional and legal infrastructure undergirding our rights to equal protection under the law.

Just a few months ago, Judicial Watch filed a class action lawsuit

RIGHTS AND FREEDOMS IN PERIL

against Evanston, Illinois, on behalf of six individuals over the city's use of race as an eligibility requirement for a reparations program that makes $25,000 payments to black residents and descendants of black residents who lived in Evanston between the years 1919 and 1969.

The class action, civil rights lawsuit challenges, "on Equal Protection grounds Defendant City of Evanston's use of race as an eligibility requirement for a program that makes $25,000 payments to residents and direct descendants of residents of the city five-plus decades if not more than a century ago. Plaintiffs seek a judgment declaring Defendant's use of race to be unconstitutional. Plaintiffs also seek an injunction enjoining Defendant from continuing to use race as a requirement for receiving payment under the program and request that the Court award them and all class members damages in the amount of $25,000 each."

Through a series of resolutions, the Evanston City Council created a program to provide $25,000 cash payments to residents who lived in Evanston between 1919 and 1969 and their children, grandchildren, and great-grandchildren.

The program violates the Equal Protection Clause of the Fourteenth Amendment because:

> Remedying societal discrimination is not a compelling
> governmental interest. Richmond v. J.A. Croson Co., 488 U.S.
> 469, 505 (1989); see also Regents of Univ. of Cal. v. Bakke,
> 438 U.S. 265, 307 ((1978) (opinion of Powell, J.) (describing
> "societal discrimination" as "an amorphous concept of injury
> that may be ageless in its reach into the past.") Remedying
> discrimination from 55 to 105 years ago or remedying
> discrimination experienced at any time by an individual's
> parents, grandparents, or great grandparents has not been
> recognized as a compelling governmental interest . . .

Defendant also has not and cannot demonstrate that its use of a race as an eligibility requirement is narrowly tailored. Among other shortcomings, Defendant's use of race as a proxy for experiencing discrimination between 1919 and 1969 does not limit eligibility to persons who actually experienced discrimination during that relevant time period and therefore is overinclusive. Defendant also failed to consider race-neutral alternatives, such as requiring prospective recipients show that they or their parents, grandparents, or great-grandparents actually experienced housing discrimination during the relevant time period because of an Evanston ordinance, policy, or procedure, as Defendant requires for the third group of prospective recipients. Nor did Defendant take into account race-neutral anti-discrimination remedies before adopting its race-based eligibility requirement.

The first group of persons eligible for the $25,000 payments are current Evanston residents who identify as black or African American and were at least eighteen years of age between 1919 and 1969. Evanston refers to this group as "ancestors."

The second group are individuals who identify as black or African American who are at least eighteen years of age and have at least one parent, grandparent, or great-grandparent who identifies (or identified) as black or African American, lived in Evanston for any period between 1919 and 1969, and was at least eighteen at the time. Evanston refers to this group as "direct descendants." A "direct descendant" is not required to be a current resident of Evanston to receive the payment.

Judicial Watch states in the lawsuit: "At no point in the application process are persons in the first and second groups required to present evidence that they or their ancestors experienced housing discrimination or otherwise suffered harm because of an unlawful Evanston ordinance, policy, or procedure or some other unlawful act or series of acts by Evanston between 1919 and 1969. In effect, Evanston is using race as a proxy for having experienced discrimination during this time period."[18]

The city committed $20 million to this nakedly racist program.

The Evanston, Illinois's, "reparations" program is nothing more than a ploy to redistribute tax dollars to individuals based on race.

This scheme unconstitutionally discriminates against anyone who does not identify as black or African American. This class action, civil rights lawsuit will be a historic defense of our colorblind Constitution.

The Left is nervous about our lawsuit because they know we're right on the law and they fear an adverse court ruling against the Evanston scheme could ruin their national plans to unmake our economy by redistributing wealth under the guise of racial reparations.

America is not a perfect country. Parts of our past didn't measure up to our founding ideals. But we must get away from the race-based spoils system that emerged in recent decades and move toward real equality under law. Critical Race Theory, married to the communist vision of "equity," has produced a monster that promises to devour all our progress and set us all against each other in a radical system that would trample our rights under woke racism, favoritism, and segregation.

CHAPTER 4

THE COVID COVERUP

From the very beginning of the Covid-19 pandemic, people demanded to know where this deadly virus came from. But the media, "experts," and certain political figures didn't allow for an open investigation into its source. In fact, they did the opposite: they shut down debate and advanced a narrative that soon fell apart.

Suspiciously, experts around the world quickly determined that the virus almost certainly came from animals, and had likely jumped from bats to humans, though the precise route of transmission was unclear. Early reports centered on the Chinese city of Wuhan, where the first cases of infection were identified.

Experts pointed to the local Huanan Seafood Market, a so-called "wet market," where local people could buy live animals for consumption or as pets. Among the animals sold at the market were raccoon dogs, porcupines, weasels, minks, bamboo rats, and other exotic species. Reports indicated that workers at the Huanan Seafood Market were among the first to get sick.

The explanation wasn't entirely implausible. Bats are mammals and carry a lot of viruses, but since they don't have an inflammatory response to viral infection, they rarely get sick or die from these infections. Bats don't acquire immunity to viruses, so they can get infected and re-infected again and again, making them an incubator for new strains and mutations. Bats also live a long time relative to their size, and because they fly around, they come into contact with both birds and other mammals. They are an ideal "vector" of transmission of disease between species.

The Huanan Seafood Market in Wuhan did not have bats for sale, but initial reports conjectured that there had likely been some sort of contact or contamination that led the virus to jump from a bat to another animal, and then to a person, probably a worker in the market. This quickly became the official answer to the question of where this new, highly contagious and apparently deadly virus had originated. The narrative was quickly set that it originated in bats and made first contact with humans at the Wuhan wet market.

But not everyone was satisfied with this account, especially when some dissenting voices pointed out that Wuhan is home to a specialized lab called the "Wuhan Institute of Virology," which specializes in the study of coronaviruses. Coronaviruses are viruses that have protein units that jut from their surfaces, like spikes, enabling them to bind to cells. The spikes make the viruses look like crowns, hence the name "coronavirus."

In 2003, the Chinese government decided to locate the nation's only biosafety level-4 laboratory at the Wuhan Institute of Virology, less than ten miles away from the now-famous wet market. Level-4 is highest degree of biocontainment for the study and storage of infectious pathogens. They have airtight chambers and airlocks, negative pressure laboratories, chemical showers and "space suits" for lab personnel, and all the rest of the scary stuff you have seen in movies from *The Andromeda Strain* to *Outbreak*.

The fact that the Wuhan Institute of Virology, which focused on the study and manipulation of bat viruses, happened to be in the same city where a bat virus broke out into the human population, eventually infecting hundreds of millions or billions of people, and killing 7 million of them, made a leak from the lab into the surrounding community at least something to consider as a possibility.

Initially, in early 2020, there was some open discussion of the question in the American media. Did the virus come from a lab, the "lab leak hypothesis," or was it through zoonosis, having jumped naturally from an animal source to humans?

This should have been an open debate. But in the context of Donald Trump's presidency and the upcoming election, the question of Covid's origins quickly became an ideological litmus test. Trump called coronavirus the "China virus," because, as he explained, rightly, "it came from China."

For this observation, Democratic politicians and their allies in media, government, and academia denounced Trump and accused him of promoting a hateful narrative that would lead to anti-Asian violence. Of course, that was also the same time that Covid, an epidemic that plainly started in China, was declared a national emergency in the United States. You didn't have to take all your news from Donald Trump to put two and two together and figure out where the virus had originated.

"Don't attach locations or ethnicity to the disease, this is not a 'Wuhan Virus,' 'Chinese Virus' or 'Asian Virus,'" the World Health Organization wrote in a February 2020 bulletin. Fair enough, but almost every serious epidemic or contagious disease we know of is named after the place it was first identified. We all know about the Spanish Flu, Rocky Mountain spotted fever, Ebola, Lyme disease, Zika, and the West Nile virus. So what was the big deal about calling the biggest epidemic in living memory after where it came from?

Within a few months, the issue of Covid's origins was taboo. If you wondered—as Trump evidently did—whether the virus came from a lab, then you were deemed a racist conspiracy theorist. On the other hand, if you agreed with Dr. Anthony Fauci, who insisted that the virus had a natural origin, then you were on the side of "Science."

In April 2020, NPR reported, "Scientists dismiss the idea that the coronavirus pandemic was caused by the accident in a lab. They believe the close interactions of people with wildlife worldwide are a far more likely culprit." Two years later, *Scientific American* took the position that discussion of the lab-leak shows how "a relatively narrow conspiracy theory can expand to endanger entire groups of people and categories of scientific research—jeopardizing both lives and lifesaving science."

The magazine went on to explain that "when Trump baldly pointed the finger at China in the earliest days of the pandemic, unfortunate consequences followed. The proliferation of xenophobic rhetoric has been linked to a striking increase in anti-Asian hate crimes." But Trump's accusation, according to *Scientific American*, had even worse effects, because it "also led to a vilification of the WIV and some of its Western collaborators, as well as partisan attempts to defund certain types of research (such as 'gain of function' research) that are linked with the presumed engineering of SARS-CoV-2."

Imagine that—Trump "vilified" a Chinese laboratory, and his rhetoric fed "partisan attempts" to defund "certain types of research" that may have links "with the presumed engineering" of the deadly virus that shut down the world economy.

How is asking questions about bioengineering deadly viruses "partisan"? What's the political angle on wanting to know whether Covid was designed in a taxpayer-funded laboratory? Well, it turns out that asking those questions threatened some very powerful people.

............,......

The almost fanatic effort to reject the "lab origin" theory was as much about protecting US government agencies and other interests as it was about protecting China from criticism.

As the Wuhan Institute received significant federal funding for what is now understood to be "gain of function" research, it becomes

106

clear why certain gatekeepers would have wanted to turn the public eye away from the "lab origin" theory. Because if Covid-19 were indeed developed in the lab, it would have likely been developed with the help of the US taxpayer!

"Gain of function" research is when scientists take a naturally occurring virus and experiment with it in order to make it worse than it is. Researchers may make it more contagious, hardier, or deadlier. This sounds totally crazy, but its proponents offer a rationale that you are free to take or leave: Viruses mutate in nature and develop deadly characteristics without human intervention. When new, unfamiliar viruses attack human populations, scientists are taken by surprise. Therefore, the smart thing to do is get ahead of evolution and create superviruses under controlled laboratory conditions, so we can figure out how best to fight them.

If this sounds something like the beginning of a dystopian zombie movie, you're not far off. It was horrifying news that the United States had been deeply involved with funding this Frankenvirus research. Ties between Dr. Anthony Fauci—the face of the government's response to the pandemic—Chinese virology experts, the World Health Organization, and Peter Daszak, a British zoologist and head of the EcoHealth Alliance, described a mysterious and global shadow public health establishment.

When news of the Wuhan lab and the type of experimental research that was conducted there began to spread, Americans began to question the official narrative about the true origins of the virus. Elements of the deep state moved to foreclose discussion by calling it conspiratorial, racist, and anti-scientific. Anthony Fauci went before Congress multiple times and swore under oath that the United States government had never funded "gain of function" research in Wuhan, parsing words and redefining standard terminology to obscure the facts. Many have suggested his testimony was false at worst and misleading at best.

Judicial Watch resolved to uncover the truth of the matter, and filed a number of FOIA suits to obtain access to emails and records, communications, contracts, and agreements between the Department of Health and Human Services and the Wuhan Institute of Virology. (The suits specifically sought records about NIH grants that benefitted the Wuhan Institute of Virology.)

Those records included an "urgent for Dr. Fauci" email chain that cites ties between the Wuhan lab and the taxpayer-funded EcoHealth Alliance.

(Further confirming the transnational effort to give China a seat at the table [and the resulting ability to control information about Covid-19], the government emails also report that the foundation of US billionaire Bill Gates worked closely with the Chinese government to pave the way for Chinese-produced medications to be sold outside China and help "raise China's voice of governance by placing representatives from China on important international counsels as high level commitment from China.")

The records also included a January 6, 2020, "Wuhan Pneumonia Update" report that details how Peter Daszak, president of EcoHealth Alliance, was tied to the Wuhan lab and was "funded for work to understand how coronaviruses evolve and jump to human populations."

Judicial Watch investigations forced the government to release troves of data demonstrating that the United States public health infrastructure had been working hand in glove with China to research bat viruses, contrary to public statements by Anthony Fauci and other top officials. Dr. Ping Chen, a top Fauci employee based in China, wrote:

> You can ask [NIAID Human Coronavirus, Rhinovirus
> Research Program Officer] Erik Stemmy for the grant awarded
> to the EcoHealth in NYC who collaborates with Dr. Shi,
> Zhengli in Wuhan Institute of Virology (WIV), who has been
> doing coronavirus research in cave bats in China. Erik would
> know what exactly NIH funding supports.

This email was part of a January 23, 2020, exchange with the subject line "Urgent for Dr. Fauci: China's lab for studying SARS and Ebola is in Wuhan." A separate email in the chain authored by Melinda Haskins, a senior NIAD official, asks senior officials to "confirm the exact nature of our support to the Wuhan Institute of Virology/ Biosafety Lab," sharing a 2017 *Daily Mail* article warning that a virus might escape the facility.[1]

So as early as January 2020, high-level discussions acknowledged the possibility that a virus contained in the special Chinese lab in Wuhan could have leaked into the general population. Long before any "conspiracy theorist" dreamed of the possibility, government officials recognized this as a possible explanation that they had to thwart.

We uncovered more emails that pointed to the disturbing possibility that US taxpayer funds were implicated in the origins of the Covid pandemic. A January 6, 2020, email exchange on "coronavirus countermeasures" includes a "Wuhan Pneumonia Update" report prepared by NIH/DMID. The report provides important background information on "Wuhan Pneumonia" (I guess the NIAID people hadn't yet been told that it was racist and xenophobic to refer to the disease by the city of origin). The report also details a NIH coronavirus grant "portfolio" that funded thirteen basic science research grants, two treatment research grants, and five vaccination research grants related to coronavirus. The report reveals that several sites were located in China, researching viruses strikingly similar to Covid-19:

> Peter Daszak (R01A|110964-06) is funded for work to understand how coronaviruses evolve and jump to human populations, with an emphasis on bat CoVs and high-risk populations at the human-animal interface. Main foreign sites are in China (including co-investigators at the Wuhan Institute of Virology).

The report notes that one of the grants, made to Fang Li, "is funded to investigate the receptor recognition and cell entry in coronaviruses using structural approaches using spike proteins in complex with receptors. This award found the first evidence of a MERS-related CoV that uses the human receptor and provides evidence of a natural recombination event between bat CoVs." This is a wordy way to describe gain of function research.

We kept at the government to reveal emails, reports, and communications relating to the lab in Wuhan and research into bat and other animal viruses. In early July 2021—the same time many Americans were being forced to undergo vaccination to participate in routine life—Judicial Watch obtained a significant cache of documents revealing significant collaborations and funding that began in 2014.

These new records reveal that NIAID gave nine China-related grants to Peter Daszak's EcoHealth Alliance to research coronavirus emergence in bats, which included a specific sub-grant for the Wuhan lab itself.

These records also include an email (sent to Dr. Fauci) from the vice director of the Wuhan Lab asking an NIH official for help finding disinfectants for decontamination of airtight suits and indoor surfaces. Apparently the Chinese containment facility was such a mess that they couldn't obtain their own anti-bacterial wipes.

The documents provided additional confirmation that the United States government was funding this dangerous research in China. A World Health Day announcement lists "successful activities" of the US-China collaboration that included "detailed surveillance throughout China and in other countries on the emergence of coronaviruses" and NIH's receipt of influenza samples from China to "assess risks associated with emerging variants for pandemic and zoonotic threat."

The records further show that, in 2018, Dr. Ping Chen, the NIAID representative in China, learned of a "type of new flu vaccine using nano-technology from China's Wuhan Institute of Virology" and discovered that the Chinese had blocked all internet links to reports on the new technology. This led Chen to write an urgent "night note" to US government officials. The note said, "The intranasal nano-vaccine can target broad-spectrum flu viruses and induces robust immune responses." In light of the subsequent covid contagion, one can't help but wonder if this secretive vaccine program was more about biologic weapons development than the public health.

The documents even included a picture of the Wuhan facility building. The documents read as if Dr. Chen, Fauci's person in China, were an amateur spy. Unable to take pictures in the lab, she sent along a touristy photo she took of the lab building.

The emails didn't only show that American public health officials were funding research into coronaviruses in China, research that included dangerous and controversial gain of function work. The new documents also showed that researchers at the Chinese laboratories expressed serious concerns about lab safety conditions. Judicial Watch obtained a 2016 email of "high importance" that senior NIH and NIAD circulated amongst themselves from Wuhan Institute of Virology Vice Director Yuan Zhiming, with the subject line "asking for help."

Zhiming's plea for assistance is worth quoting in full:

I am writing to you to ask your help. Our laboratory is under operation without pathogens, and we are now looking for the disinfectants for decontamination of airtight suits and surface decontamination indoor decontamination. We have tried several ones do [sic] determine their antiviral efficacy and corrosion to pipeline and wastewater treatment equipment. Unfortunately, we have found a good candidate. I hope you can give us some help, to give us some suggestion for the choice of disinfectants used in P4 laboratory.

What kind of disinfectants for decontamination of airtight protective clothes?

What kind of disinfectants for surface decontamination in door [*sic*]?

What kind of disinfectants for air decontamination in door [*sic*]?

What kind of disinfectants for infectious materials indoor?

What is the approval procedure for the choice of disinfectants in laboratory?

I am sorry to disturb you and I really hope you could give us some suggestion and cooment [sic].

> Best regards and looking forward to seeing you in Wuhan.
>
> Yuan Zhiming

In 2016, only three years before a new Covid virus broke out in Wuhan, the Wuhan Institute of Virology—China's only level-4 biosecurity lab—was imploring NIH for help in basic decontamination procedures.[2]

That's not to say they shouldn't have asked. In fact, it's great that the Chinese were so concerned and transparent about the hygiene standards at their top virology laboratory. But why was the United States government funding this lab and using it as an offshore facility for highly sensitive and dangerous experimentation, when they knew it had major issues with safety and decontamination?

Dr. Fauci avoided answering these basic questions. In a series of Senate hearings and media interviews he said repeatedly that his department had no involvement with gain of function viral experiments in Wuhan. In May 2021 Fauci told the Senate, "The NIH has not ever and does not now fund gain of function research in the Wuhan Institute of Virology."

But this was, at the very least, dishonest.

In December 2021, Judicial Watch discovered what appeared to be a smoking gun. We received 221 pages of records from the Department of Health and Human Services that included a grant application for research involving the coronavirus submitted in 2018. The grant application appears to describe "gain of function" research involving RNA extractions from bats, experiments on viruses, attempts to develop a chimeric virus, and efforts to genetically manipulate the full-length bat coronavirus.[3]

Fauci's allies in the press like to say that their hero didn't exactly lie about NIH funding of gain of function research in China because, technically speaking, the money was largely funneled through other entities, such as Peter Daszak's EcoHealth Alliance. They also, following Fauci, confuse the issue by fudging the definition of "gain of function" and hinging it on the relative success or failure of the experiment.

For instance, the *Washington Post* awarded Senator Rand Paul "Two Pinocchios" for his May 2021 claim to Dr. Fauci that "For years, Dr. Ralph Baric, a virologist in the US, has been collaborating with Dr. Shi Zhengli of the Wuhan Virology Institute, sharing his discoveries about how to create super viruses. This gain of function research has been funded by the NIH." The *Post* backed Fauci's denials by explaining,

> . . . is there evidence that NIH funded such gain of function research at WIV? To some extent, that depends on the definition of gain of function, which, as we noted, is open to dispute.

However, the *Post* concludes, the money that the NIH had fed through to the Wuhan Institute of Virology funded general study of "coronavirus diversity," not gain of function research specifically.

That is like saying the money you gave to a criminal on his way to rob a bank was so he could buy lunch for his kids, not bullets for his gun. But money, as we all know, is fungible. NIH was, either directly or indirectly, funding the laboratory that was trying to turn bat coronaviruses into contagious and deadly viruses that could infect and kill people.

And what exactly were these grants funding? Well, that's where things get interesting. In a "Notice of Award" dated July 13, 2020, the NIH increased the amount of NIH money going to Peter Daszak's firm, EcoHealth Alliance, by $369,819 for Daszak's project "Understanding the Risk of Bat Coronavirus Emergence."

The site locations in an EcoHealth grant application submitted November 5, 2018, for coronavirus research included EcoHealth Alliance in New York City, the University of North Carolina in Chapel Hill, the Wuhan Institute of Virology, and the Institute of Pathogen Biology in Beijing, China. Among the aims are experiments that require and invite gain of function techniques. (One of the dirty little secrets of gain of function research is that has been happening here—all over the country!)

"We will use S protein sequence data, infectious clone technology, in vitro and in vivo infection experiments and analysis of receptor binding to test the hypothesis that % divergence thresholds in S protein sequences predict spillover potential."

In a description of the Wuhan lab, the writers push the expertise of the Wuhan operation: "The Wuhan Institute of Virology is a World Health Organization collaborating center" and had a "long-time (>15 years) partnership with EcoHealth Alliance."

In the "Application for Federal Assistance," for the project "Understanding the Risk of Bat Coronavirus Emergence," the costs for the first year (2019–2020) of the EcoHealth Alliance project application totaled $736,996.

The second year (2020–2021) costs total $712,441.

The third year (2021–2022) costs total $712,441.

The fourth year (2022–2023) costs total $712,441.

The fifth year (2023-2024) costs total $712,441.

This disclosure by Judicial Watch was the first time the American people had access to the details of the gain of function research paid for and planned by Fauci's agency.

The monies included allowing Wuhan to run a bat virus factory by "running RNA extractions for 1,000 bats per year (two samples per bat: rectal and blood) in each year of the project," costing $6,214 per year. The Wuhan Institute of Virology also requested "support for in vitro experiments using pseudoviruses carrying the spike proteins . . . or live viruses in cell lines of different origins, binding affinity assays between the spike proteins . . . and different cellular receptor molecules, and humanized mice experiments." Humanized mice experiments would be a red-flag for many but not for the federal government. The grant applicants make no doubt their work necessarily includes gain of function: "In collaboration with Ralph Baric (UNC), we used the SARS-CoV reverse genetics system . . . to generate a chimeric virus with a mouse-adapted SARS-CoV backbone expressing SHC014 S protein with 10% sequence divergence from SARS-DoV S. This chimera replicated in human airway epithelium, using the human ACE2 receptor to enter cells . . . Thus, **SARS-CoVs with diverse variants of SL-CoV S protein without deletions in the RBD can use human ACE2 as receptor for cell entry.**" [Emphasis in original.]

"Chimeric" in normal language means something fanciful or imaginary. But in biology, "chimeric" means "a single organism composed of cells with more than one distinct genotype."

In other words, a monster.[4]

In a section titled "P3CO Research," the applicants wrote: "Recognizing the implementation of new gain of function research guidelines under P3CO [Potential Pandemic Pathogen Care and Oversight], SARS-CoV and MERS-CoV are subject to these guidelines, and as such, reverse genetic studies are subject to review . . . **Importantly, we are not**

proposing to genetically manipulate SARS-CoV over the course of this proposal. However, we are proposing to genetically manipulate the full length bat SARSr-CoV WIV1 strain molecular clone during the course of the proposal, which is not a select agent, has not been shown to cause human infections, and has not been shown to be transmissible between humans." [Emphasis in original.] The government-funded scientists are essentially saying they can create new and dangerous viruses because they won't supposedly be able to infect humans.

However, in July 2020, HHS wrote a letter to EcoHealth Alliance regarding funding:

[T]he NIH has received reports that the Wuhan Institute of Virology (WIV), a subrecipient of EcoHealth Alliance under R01AI110964, has been conducting research at its facilities in China that pose serious bio-safety concerns and, as a result, create health and welfare threats to the public in China and other countries, including the United States.

We have concerns that WIV has not satisfied safety requirements under the award, and that EcoHealth Alliance has not satisfied its obligations to monitor the activities of its subrecipient to ensure compliance.

Therefore, effective the date of this letter, July 8, 2020, NIH is suspending all activities . . . until such time as these concerns have been addressed to NIH's satisfaction.

So in July 2020, the US Department of Health and Human Services acknowledged that research funded at the dodgy bat virus lab in Wuhan posed "health and welfare threats" to the world, and so the NIH was "suspending" its activities with Wuhan Institute of Virology.[5]

Yet one year later, in July 2021, Fauci praised the Chinese scientists, telling Fox News, "it was research that was highly recommended by peer review, our United States peer reviews. It got a very high score in the peer review system. The purpose of the research was very, very clear. It was to try to determine what was out there in the bat population that might be ultimately risky for us. It was research that was done by qualified people."

These findings prove definitively that US tax dollars were dishonestly used by Fauci's agency to fund "gain of function" coronavirus research. It is beyond question that the United States government had a long-standing relationship with a lab in Wuhan, which we essentially built, and from which we conducted long-range research into how to turn bat viruses deadly.

Maybe there's good reason to do this. I'm not a biologist or an epidemiologist. But it's highly suspicious that when things suddenly went sideways in Wuhan at the end of 2019, the entire US scientific and media establishment quashed any discussion of a laboratory origin for the novel coronavirus, and waved a series of lies in the faces of the American people. Fauci and all of his people knew early on in the pandemic they had funded gain of function research in the very lab from which Covid may have originated. Yet, they downplayed and shut down any serious debate about this and sat silently by as millions of Americans were censored, doctors attacked, and scientific inquiry suppressed related to the "lab leak theory."

We thought we had the Fauci agency dead to rights on the funding of gain of function research relatively early on in the pandemic, but then an even bigger smoking gun emerged in April 2023 when the government gave us documents showing they gave EcoHealth money in 2013 (!) to work on mutant coronaviruses in China. That's right: mutant coronaviruses.

I must confess that it never occurred to me to call the viruses resulting from gain of function "mutants," but the Fauci/EcoHealth/ Wuhan team did! The research, which was funded with millions of tax dollars, went on for years. The material reads like a recipe for creating a dangerous pathogen.

Judicial Watch and other gain of function critics were just vindicated when the Biden administration shut off funding for EcoHealth and Wuhan gain of function research and debarred them from future funding over its gain of function chicanery. Indeed, Dr. Peter Daszak, the head of EcoHealth, is facing proceedings that may result in his personally never being able to receive taxpayer funding again!

But the stupidity continues. Our government is still funding lab research into deadly pathogens in countries such as Ukraine, where the dissolute second sons of the rich and powerful go to sell influence and scam hefty salaries on the basis of their well-connected relations. Not to mention that Ukraine is in the middle of a major war.

Shortly after Russia invaded Ukraine in February 2022, the question of US funding of Ukrainian bioweapons research was raised by some conservative commenters. It turns out that, after the fall of the Soviet Union, American scientists went to Ukraine to help them contain and "secure" old bioweapons.

It should have taken a year or two to safely dispose of dangerous and obsolete Soviet biowarfare labs and weapons. But instead, the US chose to continue the operation of the labs. As in Wuhan, the Ukrainian labs are run ostensibly to stay on top of the *threat* of biowarfare, not to develop weapons. For example, the US Embassy in Ukraine claims the US Department of Defense's Biological Threat Reduction Program is purely for bio-threat reduction.

But in November 2022, Judicial Watch uncovered records from the Defense Threat Reduction Agency (DTRA), a component of the US Department of Defense, revealing that the United States funded anthrax laboratory activities in a Ukrainian biolab in 2018. Dozens of pages are completely redacted, and many others are heavily redacted. The records show over $11 million in funding for the Ukraine biolabs program in 2019.

Undersecretary of State for Political Affairs Victoria Nuland—an architect of the Iraq War under George W. Bush and Obama's point person for the 2014 coup in Ukraine—admitted to the US Senate Foreign Relations Committee in 2022, "Ukraine has biological research facilities, which in fact we are now quite concerned that Russian forces may be seeking to gain control of, so we are working with the Ukrainians on how they can prevent any of those research materials from falling into the hands of Russian forces, should they approach."

Around the same time, the New York Post reported that— surprise!— Hunter Biden helped secure funds for a US biolab contractor in Ukraine.

Is the US using Ukrainian labs to weaponize anthrax, or is it just refining surveillance measures in case Russia uses anthrax as a weapon? Given what we know now about NIH-funded gain of research into bat viruses in China, would it be enormously surprising to discover that similar types of experimentation are going on in Ukraine?

"Dual use" research is commonly discussed in regard to nuclear capabilities. Labs and scientists can work on developing beneficial uses of nuclear energy to feed the power grid, and the same research can simultaneously be used to advance weapons programs. The fact that the US is heavily invested in anthrax labs in Ukraine would be problematic even if the country weren't being bombed by Russia.

These documents Judicial Watch uncovered shed needed light on US involvement in the management and handling of pathogens in Ukrainian biolabs. But we certainly need the government to be forthcoming about what's really going on.

First up, there's more than enough evidence to commence a criminal investigation into the fraud confirmed by the Biden administration tied to Fauci agency funding of gain of function research in China. Judicial Watch uncovered that the FBI was investigating this issue back in 2020, but no law enforcement steps have been evident since then.

The cover-up of this scandal required a massive suppression of speech and scientific inquiry. To this day, we still don't have a clue about how Covid-19 emerged. It is bad enough the Chinese government suppressed any inquiry. But perhaps the real outrage is that the Chinese government cover-up was helped along directly and indirectly by the US media, social media censors, politicians, and self-interested officials such as Anthony Fauci.

CHAPTER 5

AN ELECTION UNLIKE ANY OTHER

The 2020 election, according to the Left, was totally different from the 2016 election. The 2016 election, we were told, was compromised, rigged, and stolen. Russian conspirators went "all out," according to *Time* magazine, to interfere with Hillary Clinton's anticipated victory. The Russian government and its agents—possibly including members of the Trump campaign if not Donald Trump himself—forged and executed a game plan to steal the election.

Top-level Obama appointees agreed that only Vladimir Putin himself could have orchestrated the plot. On January 6, 2017, just two weeks before Trump would take the oath of office, the Director of National Intelligence James Clapper delivered a classified "Intelligence Community Assessment" into "Russian Activities and Intentions in Recent US Elections."

The "Key Judgments" of the report are stark:

Russian efforts to influence the 2016 US presidential election
represent the most recent expression of Moscow's longstanding
desire to undermine the US-led liberal democratic order,
but these activities demonstrated a significant escalation in

directness, level of activity, and scope of effort compared to previous operations.

We assess Russian President Vladimir Putin ordered an influence campaign in 2016 aimed at the US presidential election. Russia's goals were to undermine public faith in the US democratic process, denigrate Secretary Clinton, and harm her electability and potential presidency. We further assess Putin and the Russian Government developed a clear preference for President-elect Trump. We have high confidence in these judgments.

We also assess Putin and the Russian Government aspired to help President-elect Trump's election chances when possible by discrediting Secretary Clinton and publicly contrasting her unfavorably to him. All three agencies agree with this judgment. CIA and FBI have high confidence in this judgment; NSA has moderate confidence.[1]

Pretty damning stuff. According to the highest levels of the US "intelligence community," the dictator of Russia wanted to install Donald Trump in the White House by effectively stealing the election from Hillary Clinton, who by all accounts was the most qualified and credible candidate for the presidency in the history of the republic.

Exactly how the Russians managed to steal the election—and the extent of Trump's direct involvement—was yet unknown. But, from the perspective of early 2017, it was just a matter of time before we figured it all out.

In contrast to the blighted election of 2016, however, the election of 2020 was a rose in bloom. On November 13—just ten days after the election in which Joe Biden received a record-breaking 81 million votes—the Associated Press reported that "a broad coalition of top government and industry officials is declaring that the Nov. 3 voting and the following count unfolded smoothly with no more than the usual minor hiccups."

According to a joint statement written primarily by the Cybersecurity and Infrastructure Security Agency, and joined by a number of other public and private entities, including the Electronic Registration Information Center (ERIC) and Democracy Works, the 2020 election was "the most secure in American history."

The joint statement continued, "There is no evidence that any voting system deleted or lost votes, changed votes, or was in any way compromised."[2]

So in just four years, the results of a national election went from the most compromised to the most secure in our nation's history. The same people who questioned the results of the 2016 election castigated those who expressed reasonable doubts about new procedures introduced in the 2020 election.

Little evidence of result-determinative election fraud had emerged in the first week or two after the election. But to many it seemed a bit premature for a major government agency—a key member of the "intelligence community"— to announce that the 2020 election was definitively the most secure in American history.

Especially when we know, without a doubt, that it wasn't.

Election integrity has been a core issue for Judicial Watch for decades. Nothing is more important to the functioning of a democratic system than public confidence that voting is conducted in a clear and transparent manner. Americans can take losing in stride—we may not like it, but fair is fair. But what Americans cannot abide is the sense that, as in many low-trust, corrupt societies, voting is meaningless because the election process and the count are dirty.

Soviet dictator Joseph Stalin is credited as having said, "It's not who votes that counts; but who counts the votes," or words to that effect. (Experts say there's no evidence that Stalin ever said it, but the sentiment definitely fits.) Legendary nineteenth-century political cartoonist Thomas Nast drew a picture of New York City's "Boss" Tweed—the king of the Tammany Hall political machine that ran Gotham for a century—leaning against a ballot box labeled "In Counting There Is Strength," and saying, "As long as I count the votes, what are you going to do about it?"

So voting and election integrity are extremely important, even if they smack of "goo-goo" good government wonkery. Voting rolls, precinct workers, petition signatures, and the rest of the machinery of election processing aren't sexy, but if they don't work—or even if they appear not to be working—public confidence in our political system will collapse.

A major change to the way our elections are handled was passed shortly after Bill Clinton took office. The National Voter Registration Act of 1993 was designed to make it easier to register people to vote, and thus to increase turnout. Known as the "Motor Voter" law, the NVRA requires states to offer registration at motor vehicle agencies (and many other government agencies that serve the public); to make mail-in voter registration possible; and to allow welfare and disability recipients to register to vote at public assistance offices.

The Left had long sought to get more people registered to vote, operating on the assumption that stubborn non-registrants tended to be racial minorities or poor, and thus more likely to vote for Democrats. Republican opposition to the legislation, while easy to caricature as "voter suppression," was grounded in what President George H. W. Bush described in his 1992 veto of an earlier version of the NRVA, as exposing "the election process to an unacceptable risk of fraud and corruption without any reason to believe that it would increase electoral participation to any significant degree."

Bush was right that electoral participation didn't change much after the bill came into effect. But his fraud and corruption comments were grounded in serious concerns about the integrity of voter lists. Millions of people move from one state to another every year; in 2022, according to the Census Bureau, approximately 8.2 million Americans moved and took up residency in a different state. That means that they left behind their voter registration in their old state, and—maybe— registered in a new state.

Another 3.3 million people—about 1 percent of the population— die every year. We all know the stories about how busy the Chicago cemeteries are on Election Day, and while these might just be amusing jokes about an ethically loose municipal political system, there's no doubt that deceased people remain on voter rolls, sometimes for many years.

Extrapolating the data to an entire election cycle, it's not unreasonable to estimate that as many as 45 million people may change states or die in between each presidential election. That's about a quarter of the total popular vote.

So what happens to all those defunct registrations? When most Americans move, I suspect that contacting the Board of Elections in their old precincts to alert them to remove them from the rolls is low on the list of things to do.

To allay concerns about sloppy voter rolls, the NRVA that Bill Clinton signed into law included a provision that forces states to clean up their registration lists regularly. The law "requires States to **complete** any program the purpose of which is to systematically remove the names of ineligible voters from the official list of eligible voters not later than **90 days** prior to the date of a primary election or general election for federal office. This 90 day deadline applies to state list maintenance verification activities such as general mailings and door to door canvasses."[3] [Emphasis in original.]

Cleaning up the voter rolls every two years has typically not been a high priority for state boards of elections, especially in the run-up to a primary or general election. And Judicial Watch has filed lawsuit after lawsuit to force states to comply with the law and get non-residents and the deceased off the rolls. Previous Judicial Watch lawsuits have already led to major cleanups in California, Kentucky, Indiana, and Ohio, but this is not a "one-and-done" procedure. If states fail to cull their registration lists promptly and regularly, American elections will become a farce.

It is common sense that voters who die or move away be removed from the voting rolls. But our research has shown that noncompliance with the law has resulted in extraordinarily inaccurate registration lists. And the extraordinary conditions surrounding the 2020 election created a kind of "perfect storm" for massive irregularities at the ballot box.

At the start of 2020, Judicial Watch reported that our analysis of data released by the US Election Assistance Commission (EAC) revealed there were 378 counties nationwide that had more voter registrations than citizens living there and old enough to vote. That is to say, the voter registration rates in these counties exceeded 100 percent.

These 378 counties combined had about 2.5 million registrations *above* the 100 percent registered mark. Given that our recent presidential elections have been decided by relative handfuls of voters—around 100,000 or less—across a small number of counties, the existence of millions of zombie registrations is a serious concern.

Remember that in 2016 Trump beat Hillary Clinton in Wisconsin by 22,000 votes; in Pennsylvania by 44,000 votes; and in Michigan by around 10,000 votes. Those margins made the difference in the Electoral College.

In 2020, Biden beat Trump in Georgia by 12,000 votes, in Wisconsin by 20,000 votes, and in Pennsylvania by 77,000 votes. Those margins made Biden the president. Moreover, Biden won in only 477 counties nationwide, a record low.

So 2.5 million extra registrations, in just 378 counties, is far from insignificant.

We sent the most egregious offenders letters explaining that implausibly high registration rates raise legal concerns:

An unusually high registration rate suggests that a jurisdiction is not removing voters who have died or who have moved elsewhere, as required by federal law.

Judicial Watch also considers how many registrations were ultimately removed from the voter rolls because a registrant [had moved]. If few or no voters were removed . . . the jurisdiction is obviously failing to comply . . . States must report the number of such removals to the EAC.

Judicial Watch found major voting list issues in California, Pennsylvania, North Carolina, Virginia, and Colorado.

"Dirty voting rolls can mean dirty elections and Judicial Watch will insist, in court if necessary, that states follow federal law to clean up their voting rolls," I said at the time.[4]

In February 2020 we alerted Iowa that eight of its counties had registration lists that were greater than 100 percent of the voting-age population. This amounted to about 19,000 names. Iowa is solidly red, and this total number wouldn't mean anything in a presidential election that was won by over 100,000 votes, but cleaning up the rolls is essential to maintaining confidence in American elections. "Iowa needs to undertake a serious effort to address its voting rolls," I said.

The problem exists across the country. In April 2020, Judicial Watch filed a lawsuit against North Carolina and two of its counties for failing to clean their voter rolls. According to our analysis of voter registration data, many of North Carolina's 100 counties had a combined total of nearly 1 million inactive voters on their rolls.

We argued that North Carolina, Mecklenburg County, and Guilford County failed to make reasonable efforts to remove ineligible voters from their registration rolls. Data showed that voter registration rates in a significant proportion of North Carolina's 100 counties were close to, at, or above 100 percent of their age-eligible citizenry. In fact, the entire state of North Carolina had a registration rate close to 100 percent of its age-eligible citizenry.

North Carolina's abnormally high number of inactive registrations showed that it was not removing these registrations after two general federal elections, as the law requires. According to the state's own data:

> About 17 percent of North Carolina's registrations were inactive, which was the fifth worst (highest) of the 40 states for which data were available;
>
> By way of comparison, the median state inactive rate was 9.6 percent;
>
> In 19 North Carolina counties, 20 percent or more of the registrations were inactive, and in three counties 25 percent or more were inactive.

Moreover, as of March 2020, North Carolina's own data showed it had nearly 1 million inactive registrations, and a large proportion of these registrations had shown no voting activity for more than five years—that is, since prior to November 2014.

North Carolina is slightly red—Trump won the 2020 election by a slim margin. It is vitally important for all states to get their voter rolls cleaned up in order to ensure that the only votes that are counted are legally cast in the first place.[5]

Later that same month, we sued Pennsylvania and three of its counties, which said they had removed almost no names from their lists under relevant federal laws. The lawsuit noted that the state had more than 800,000 "inactive" registrations on its voter rolls.

In the subsequent litigation, the original three counties we sued confessed that they had misstated the number of outdated registrations they removed—and that the number was actually *higher* than they originally reported. They were ultimately dismissed from the suit. What we learned at the same time, however, was that the situation in Pennsylvania was much *worse* than we initially thought. We identified *fourteen* counties that removed shockingly few registrations—in some cases, zero registrations—under the relevant NVRA procedures. We amended our complaint to sue the state and five counties. Several other Pennsylvania counties told us point blank that they only took steps to clean their voter rolls once we contacted them about whether they were doing so. And when Pennsylvania itself told us that, because of our lawsuit, it had worked with its counties to remove almost 180,000 ineligible registrants, we agreed to settle the case.

We don't carry out this work for the purpose of putting out press releases or just to note how the law is being flouted. On January 14, 2020, CBS Pittsburgh reported that because of the threat of a lawsuit from Judicial Watch, Allegheny County removed 69,000 inactive voters. David Voye, elections manager for the county, told CBS, "I would concede that we are behind on culling our rolls," and that this had "been put on the backburner."[6]

We were able to settle our federal lawsuits with North Carolina and Pennsylvania after those states, respectively, removed 430,000 and 178,000 outdated voter names.

Our concern, historically, has not been that millions of Americans are actually going back to their old place of residence so they can vote twice, or voting in the name of their deceased relatives. The concern is that the dirty voting rolls are a potential pool of names for fraudsters to use, that unlawful and poor voter roll maintenance suggests other deficiencies and election mismanagement, and that the dirty voting rolls undermine public confidence in election outcomes.

For years, Americans have been losing faith in the integrity of our electoral system. Many polls have been taken on this subject and they reach the same conclusion. The Gallup organization conducts a particularly interesting poll, which compares American attitudes with those of other countries. The poll simply asks respondents if they "have confidence" in the "honesty of elections."

In 2019, only 40 percent of Americans answered yes, while an astonishing 59 percent said no. According to Gallup, the United States has "one of the worst ratings across the world's wealthiest democracies," with only Chile and Mexico reporting statistically lower ratings. This phenomenon long predated the Covid-19 pandemic. Gallup reports that "[m]ajorities of Americans have consistently lacked confidence in the honesty of elections every year since 2012."[7]

Among the explanations for this loss of faith, we must include the public's impatience with the politicization of electoral procedure, and, in particular, with dubious objections to what are widely perceived to be commonsense election integrity measures. The most obvious example to date concerns the heated, partisan fight against voter ID laws.

A Pew Research Center study after the 2018 elections found strong, bipartisan support for voter ID, which was favored overall by 76 percent of those polled and even by a considerable majority of those identifying as Democrats (63 percent). This support is understandable in a society where one must produce identification for so many different reasons, from getting on a plane to buying prescription drugs to working out in a gym.

That voter ID laws are so often opposed, and with significant success, by the Left and Democratic Party politicians is a sad sign of the times. This opposition often relies on false claims that voter ID depress minority turnout, but this "voter suppression" is never seen in actual elections. In fact, the *Wall Street Journal* reports that "The lack of suppressive outcome explains why requiring photo ID to vote is 'favored by 77% of people of color and 80% of White adults,' to quote Gallup."[8]

Opponents of voter ID also try to flip the burden of proof, arguing in effect that, unless those favoring voter ID can prove that voter fraud is a common occurrence that costs elections, there is no justification for requiring an ID. This argument is bogus. As the Supreme Court has noted, regardless of the prevalence of fraud, states have an obvious, legitimate "interest in counting only the votes of eligible voters" and in "carefully identifying all voters participating in the election process." This interest is justified by the nature of voter fraud, which is hard to detect or punish after the fact.

Practically speaking, people who mock the voter fraud concerns reveal an unrealistic, if touching, view of human nature. People cheat at everything. They cheat at baseball. They cheat at poker. They cheat when it doesn't matter—just look at online gaming or internet chess. Indeed, they cheat at solitaire. Why would voting, which is so tied up with intense partisan feeling and enthusiasm, be exempt from cheating?

I don't know how many politicians or local poll workers you've talked to, but "behind the scenes," on both sides, they openly brag about election day shenanigans, lost ballots, duped voters, bogus petition challenges, and so forth.

And that was before Covid. Then came the pandemic, and our system of voting was turned completely upside down.

Almost as soon as lockdowns and mask mandates were put in place, politicians and journalists started fretting about elections and "voter safety." How could we expect people to vote in person when the danger of catching Covid was so acute?

States immediately began changing the rules and procedures to establish universal mail-in balloting. In California, Governor Gavin

Newsom issued an executive order in May 2020 stating that "to preserve public health in the face of the threat of Covid-19, and to ensure that the November election is accessible, secure, and safe, all Californians must be empowered to vote by mail, from the safety of their own homes." There was no longer a requirement for voters to request a ballot or cite a reason for needing to vote absentee; the state would send every registered voter a ballot.

It's worth noting that the US Constitution specifies in Article I, Section 4 that it's the role of state legislatures to decide the "Times, Places and Manner of holding Elections." While the Constitution says that Congress can supersede the states in this regard, it says nothing about letting state governors, secretaries of state, state or local election boards, or judges insert themselves into the process and alter the "Manner" of holding elections. But such orders and alterations were made throughout the country.

Automatically sending mail-in ballots to every registered voter was a real threat to the integrity of American elections. And I'm not the only one who thinks so. In 2004, former president Jimmy Carter and former Cabinet secretary and Republican White House official James A. Baker III formed the Commission on Federal Election Reform to examine the electoral process in the United States, along with leaders from the major political parties, academia, and civic groups to figure out ways to improve both ballot access and integrity.

In 2005, the Carter-Baker Commission noted the particular risks associated with absentee (mail-in) ballots:

> Absentee ballots remain the largest source of potential voter fraud. . . . Absentee balloting is vulnerable to abuse in several ways: Blank ballots mailed to the wrong address or to large residential buildings might get intercepted. Citizens who vote at home, at nursing homes, at the workplace, or in church

are more susceptible to pressure, overt and subtle, or to intimidation. Vote buying schemes are far more difficult to detect when citizens vote by mail.[9]

I agree that these are all problems. But the most obvious is indisputably the problem of sending ballots to the wrong address. I explained above how hundreds of counties across America have done a terrible job of cleaning up their voting rolls and expunging voters who have died or moved. There are many localities that have in excess of 100 percent of their voting-age population registered to vote.

But even that doesn't really get at the scope of the problem. A Pew Research Center report issued during the Obama years noted that "[a]pproximately 2.75 million people have active registrations in more than one state," that "24 million—one of every eight—active voter registrations in the United States are no longer valid or are significantly inaccurate," and that "[m]ore than 1.8 million deceased individuals are listed as active voters."[10]

Counties throughout the country have high numbers of "inactive" registrations that have not yet been canceled. A registration becomes inactive when a registrant is sent, and fails to respond to, an address confirmation notice. If that registrant does not vote or otherwise contact election officials for the next two general federal elections (from two to four years), that registration is canceled pursuant to the law. During that statutory waiting period the voter is called inactive.

What this means in reality is that California mailed out ballots indiscriminately, and almost certainly sent millions of ballots to voters who had long moved away or died.

Consider our experience in Los Angeles County, which we sued for noncompliance with the NVRA in 2017. We learned that the state of California had not been removing inactive registrations for twenty years, pursuant to a misguided accommodation reached with Janet Re-no's Justice Department. As a result, Los Angeles County by 2018 had about 1,565,000 inactive registrations—almost one-fourth of all the registrations in the county.

Stated differently, the county of Los Angeles alone had more inactive voter registrations than the state of Hawaii has people. And this is not just Judicial Watch's calculation. These inactive registrations were tallied by Los Angeles County, and were openly admitted in the agreement it signed settling the lawsuit. Some had been inactive for almost twenty years. Most had moved long ago. Tens of thousands of these inactive registrants had died. But all currently remain "registered voters."

But until all these registrations were formally processed under the NVRA, however, which would not be completed until 2022, they could still be used to cast votes in Los Angeles County. Gavin Newsom's executive order requires county officials to "transmit vote-by-mail ballots for the November 3, 2020 General Election to all voters who are . . . registered to vote in that election," making clear that "every Californian who is eligible to vote in the November 3, 2020 General Election shall receive a vote-by-mail ballot."

Under the plain terms of Governor Newsom's order, these 1.6 million inactive registrations, the vast majority of whom no longer reside in LA, received ballots. Circulating all of those live ballots, unmonitored by their original owners who have moved or died, was a massive threat to the integrity of California's 2020 vote.

What's even worse—if it can get worse—is that if mail-in ballots are sent to the addresses of inactive voters, and someone else uses the ballot to vote, at that point they will become "active" again and not subject to removal. Indeed, where states or counties are not cleaning their voter rolls, even their active registrations become outdated.

There is little doubt there is more work to be done. We just had to sue California again after we uncovered a broad failure to clean up voter rolls in dozens of California counties. It is frustrating, as California knows the NVRA requires states to "conduct a general program that makes a reasonable effort to remove" from the official voter rolls "the names of ineligible voters" who have died or changed residence. The law requires registrations to be canceled when voters fail to respond to address confirmation notices and then fail to vote in the next two general federal elections. (In 2018, the Supreme Court confirmed that such removals are mandatory.)

Indeed, California notified us in 2023 that they removed 1,207,613 ineligible voters from the rolls of Los Angeles County alone under the terms of a settlement agreement in a federal lawsuit Judicial Watch filed in 2017. But they still haven't got their act together statewide.

Our latest lawsuit details, in correspondence with Judicial Watch, California:

> admit[ted] that 21 California counties removed five or fewer
> registrations pursuant to [the NVRA] . . . for failing to
> respond to a Confirmation Notice and then failing to vote
> in two general federal elections . . . from November 2020 to
> November 2022. Sixteen of the 21 counties removed *zero* such
> registrations during this period . . . Together, these 21 counties
> reported a combined total of 11 removal (under the relevant
> NVRA law) during this two-year reporting period.[11]

Illinois's voting rolls are a mess, too. We had to sue Illinois in 2023 after discovering a total failure across the state to clean the voter rolls. An incredible 23 Illinois counties, with a combined registration list of 980,089 voters, reported removing a combined total of only 100 registrations in the previous two-year reporting period under the crucial provision of the NVRA.

One of the most basic tasks of election officials is to remove the names of dead voters from the rolls. Illinois lives up to its reputation in that regard: nineteen Illinois counties also failed to report any data regarding registrations removed because of the death of the voter!

One of the main reasons the Carter-Baker Commission identified absentee ballot fraud as "the largest source of potential voter fraud" is simple: It poses fewer risks for a person filling out and mailing a fraudulent ballot. By contrast, a person attempting "impersonation" fraud at a polling site must at least appear to cast the vote and, in consequence, may be found out and detained. "Unsupervised voting" is anathema to the very idea of clean elections.

Even so, a number of recent stories attest to mail-in ballot fraud. In West Virginia in 2020, a postal worker was indicted for manipulating eight voters' absentee ballots. In 2019, an Oakland County clerk outside Detroit, Michigan, was charged with illegally altering 193 absentee ballots. A Minneapolis, Minnesota, man was charged with helping thirteen others falsify absentee ballots ahead of the 2018 election. In 2017, a Dallas County, Texas, man was convicted after 700 mail-in ballots were witnessed and signed by a fictitious person. And recently in North Carolina's 9th Congressional District race, a scheme was run (by a Republican operative) to steal 1,200 absentee ballots and fill them out, in a race that was decided by only 900 votes.

So it's not like it never happens, and those cases were in relatively normal times, before the Left decided to impose mail-in voting on steroids on dozens of states. The total number of mail-in ballots rose from 28.8 million in 2016 to 66.4 million in 2020. And as I discussed above, something on the order of 8 million people move from state to state each year. Millions more move from one county to another within the same state, and millions of people die. With ballots being mailed out willy-nilly, we really have no reasonable assurance who voted in many states in 2020.

Even while Gavin Newsom was claiming that a dangerous pandemic necessitated mass mail-in voting so everyone could isolate themselves and not run the risk of catching Covid, he notably failed to restrict "ballot harvesting" under state law, which allows paid employees of public sector unions, among others, to go door-to-door gathering ballots from strangers, even helping those voters to fill them out.

Ballot harvesting is a classic leftist program. It sounds like something wholesome and organic, when it in fact represents the ultimate culmination of dirty machine politics. Harvesting, or "vote chasing" as it might more properly be called, allows political operatives to solicit and collect ballots from people who might otherwise not bother voting. The potential for abuse is virtually limitless.

In 2016, the California legislature massively expanded ballot harvesting. It permitted the unlimited collection of ballots by any person, even a campaign worker. They did not have to give their names or present any identification or authorization to those they visited. Ballot harvesters could be paid to collect ballots, so long as they weren't paid as a matter of piecework. The legislature also expanded the use of ballot drop-boxes and moved to discourage in-person voting.

The effect of these changes was profound. It gave rise to a new profession of "ballot brokers" who target apartment blocks or nursing homes, and stand by to "assist" residents with the filling out and delivery of the ballots. A congressional report, "Political Weaponization of Ballot Harvesting in California," notes:

> This behavior can result in undue influence in the voting
> process and destroys the secret ballot, a long-held essential
> principle of American elections intended to protect voters.
> These very scenarios are what anti-electioneering laws at polling
> locations are meant to protect against. A voter cannot wear a
> campaign button to a polling location, but a political operative
> can collect your ballot in your living room?

Furthermore, it has been reported that these ballot brokers intercept and destroy mail-in ballots of voters who traditionally vote against the brokers' preferred party. These ballot brokers are the new Tammany Hall ward bosses, controlling the votes of their harvested area. Brokers are often added to campaign payrolls based purely on the number of ballots they promise to harvest.[12]

Indeed, the 2018 congressional midterm elections in California were the first indication that ballot harvesting and mass mail-in voting were warping the political process. The night of the election, seven Republican candidates were either leading in their races, or the races were too close to call. But as weeks went on, the counting of last-minute dropped-off ballots led to outsized, statistically improbable results. As the report from the Committee on House Administration explains:

> In Orange County alone, 250,000 mailed ballots were turned in on Election Day. Orange County Registrar of Voters, Neal Kelley, indicated to the media that some individuals appeared at his office to deposit "maybe 100 or 200" ballots at a time. Maintaining and transporting hundreds of ballots is an enormous responsibility even for election officials, much less a private citizen. There is additional concern for ballot security when the individual collecting ballots can be paid by outside, nongovernment organizations, as they can in California. In the 2014 general election, California saw 4,547,705 mail-in ballots cast; that number nearly doubled to 8,302,488 in 2018. This upward trend of mail-in voting, as well as the increasing number of harvested ballots, was the intent of the California

State Assembly in 2016. In-person voting ensures safeguards that cannot be duplicated when picking up ballots.

The experience of California was felt by the whole country in 2020, when late-night mailed ballot "dumps" shifted Trump's apparent edge in Michigan, Wisconsin, and Pennsylvania toward Biden, often in suspiciously massive spikes. Rumors of trucks delivering bags of ballots to counting sites in Georgia resounded with voters whose confidence in the system was already badly shaken.

None of this is helped by the fact that whereas it used to take a few hours for all the votes to be counted, even in a national election, it has now become normal and expected that tabulating mail-in votes may add days or even weeks to the process. It is all well and good to be assured continuously that there is nothing weird about new tranches of votes emerging from the corners of California congressional districts ten days after the election, but when all the shifts tend in one direction it seems more than a little suspicious.

The fact is that then-president Trump had the votes to win the presidency on Election Day. These vote totals were changed because of unprecedented and extraordinary counting after Election Day.

Judicial Watch was ahead of the curve regarding ballot harvesting. In late September 2020, I posted on our YouTube channel a video called "**ELECTION INTEGRITY CRISIS** Dirty Voter Rolls, Ballot Harvesting & Mail-in-Voting Risks!" The twenty-six-minute video featured me discussing the vote-by-mail processes, changes to states' election procedures, ballot harvesting, and states' failures to clean up their voter rolls, among other topics.

Within two days, Akilah Jones, a California public employee who worked for the California Office of Elections Cybersecurity, communicated her dissatisfaction with our video to YouTube. Jones wrote,

Hi YouTube Reporting Team,

I am reporting the following video because it misleads community members about elections or other civic processes and misrepresents the safety and security of mail-in ballots. Thank you for your time and attention on this matter.

All the best, Akilah.

The next day, September 25, 2020, YouTube representative Andrea Holtermann replied to Jones:

Hi Akilah,

Thanks for reaching out. We will look into this and get back to you as soon as we can.

Later that same day, Judicial Watch noticed that the video had been taken down.

On September 27, 2020, YouTube and/or Google's Holtermann confirmed to Jones that Judicial Watch's video had been removed:

Hi Akilah,

Circling back on this. Thank you for raising this content to our attention, this has been removed from the platform for violating our policies. Please do not hesitate to reach out if there are any other questions or concerns you may have.

Astonishing! My video is not "misleading" about elections or civil processes in the least. Nor did it "misrepresent" the "safety and security of mail-in ballots." But this was deep in the pandemic days when any reference to "safety" was enough to stomp all over the First Amendment.

My video pointed out that, as of its production, over 50 million ballots had already been mailed to people who hadn't even asked for one, and another 40 million ballot applications had gone out to people who hadn't expressed an interest in mail-in voting.

"Vote by mail is notoriously susceptible to fraud," I explained. "If you're not voting in a polling location, where you have government officials protecting you and making sure nothing improper goes on—they can have party observers and candidate observers at the polls—it's not a perfect process but it certainly protects against voter fraud.

"But if you start mailing ballots to lists which you know are dirty, as Judicial Watch has found out, you've got a major problem. Because whether the voters are inactive or not, when you've got lists that are dirty, with names that shouldn't be there, it means that the rest of the active list is probably dirty as well. And certainly to mail out ballots blindly is irresponsible.

"I don't care if your list is 100 percent clean. This is the franchise we're talking about. Look how mobile we are. People move all the time. So a list that's clean today might not be clean tomorrow. And that's why voting in person is the best way to conduct elections."[13]

None of this is scurrilous. I didn't defame anyone or claim that there was an active effort to defraud the public on the part of any group. But YouTube or someone at its parent company Google was told by someone in a government agency in California that didn't like what Judicial Watch had to say about the open can of squirming worms that is mail-in voting, and they removed our content within a few hours.

This of course gets to a much bigger issue, which is the way in which the government pushes major tech platforms to censor the American people, and end-runs around the Constitution by pretending that all they do is make innocent requests. It's the companies that quash the discourse, you see, not the government. But of course these tech companies know how to take a hint. We have a major civil rights lawsuit over this abuse in California. This subject is also in front of the Supreme Court as I write this, and I seriously hope that the court reins in the government's use of private companies as a cat's paw to stifle speech it happens not to like.

The problems with mass mail-in balloting are numerous and confusing, to the point where it almost seems like the chaos has to be intentional. In the name of ballot access and more democracy, the forces of the Left are destroying the buttresses of our system.

Mail-in ballots are supposed to be signed, and the signature is supposed to match the signature on file with the local board of elections. Most states reject a certain percentage of mismatched signatures, and the number usually averages around 1 percent nationwide. Some states, like New York and New Jersey, typically run higher.

After the 2020 election, partisan advocates for expanded mail-in balloting acknowledged that the rate of ballot rejection for signature mismatch fell a bit from earlier elections.

But while the rate of rejected signatures may not have been immensely different in 2020, the standards for judging whether or not a signature was acceptable certainly were. In Michigan, for instance, the law required trained election officials to verify that ballot signatures "agreed" with the signatures on file. But before the 2020 election, Michigan's Democrat Secretary of State Jocelyn Benson issued a new guidance stating that ballots should be presumed to be legitimate unless there were "multiple, significant, and obvious differences" between the two signatures.

This relaxed standard meant that ballots were effectively waved through as legitimate, mostly by temporary staffers, regardless of the signature. In 2021, a Michigan court ruled that the signature verification guidance issued by Benson was invalid because it didn't conform to rule-making procedures. But as with similar illegal and ad hoc orders and rules around the country made under the cover of a health emergency, it was too little, too late.

In Georgia, the mail-ballot rejection rate dropped from 6.4 percent to only .36 percent as the result of changes to election law and lawsuit settlement with the state Democratic Party that it made more difficult to reject mailed-in ballots.

Beyond the question of the legitimacy of a specific ballot is the legal debate about when states should accept ballots. According to federal law, Election Day is the "the first Tuesday after the first Monday in November of every even-numbered year." Seems clear enough. But states have expanded "early voting" to the point that there is no longer one day, but a whole season, stretching up to fifty days before the official day of the election.

But because mail-in voting has become so widespread, it's no longer clear when the Election Season ends. Numerous states count votes that show up weeks after the election!

In May 2022, Judicial Watch filed suit against the state of Illinois on behalf of Congressman Mike Bost and two other registered Illinois voters to prevent state election officials from extending Election Day for fourteen days beyond the date established by federal law.

We argued that Illinois election law violates federal law. The complaint states:

> Despite Congress' clear statement regarding a single national
> Election Day, Illinois has expanded Election Day by extending by
> 14 days the date for receipt and counting of vote-by-mail ballots

It's astounding that current Illinois election law allows vote-by-mail ballots received up to fourteen days "after the polls close on Election Day" to be counted as if they were cast and received on or before Election Day. Illinois law also provides that "[e]ven vote-by-mail ballots without postmarks shall be counted if received up to 14 calendar days after Election Day if the ballots are dated on or before Election Day."

The old joke about "voting early and often" in Chicago can now credibly be amended to "vote early, often . . . and late, too."

Judicial Watch's lawsuit notes:

> The Board . . . advised that the number of ballots received after Election Day through November 17, 2020, could materially affect the unofficial election results.
>
> . . . .
>
> [Illinois' own data indicates that] Illinois received 266,417 vote-by-mail ballots statewide during the period from November 3rd through November 17th.
>
> [M]ost of the 266,417 vote-by-mail ballots were received after Election Day, which would mean that as many as 4.4% of votes cast in 2020 were received *after* Election Day. [Emphasis in original.]

Judicial Watch argues that holding voting open for fourteen days past Election Day violates the constitutional rights of voters and candidates:

> By counting untimely and illegal ballots received after Election Day and diluting Plaintiffs' timely cast and received ballots, Defendants, acting under color of Illinois law, have deprived and are depriving Plaintiffs of rights protected under the First

Amendment and 14th Amendment to the U.S. Constitution in violation of 42 U.S.C. § 1983.

"We are supposed to have an Election Day, not Election Weeks—or months. Illinois's fourteen-day extension of Election Day beyond the date set by Congress is illegal, violates the civil rights of voters, and encourages fraud," I said when we filed the suit.[14]

We also filed a similar lawsuit against Mississippi, a Republican-controlled state, that counts ballots received up to five days after Election Day.

States vary widely on the question of acceptance of late ballots. Connecticut has a sensible rule that ballots "must be received by the close of polls on Election Day. Hand-delivered ballots must be received the day before an election if delivered by the voter and by the close of polls on Election Day if delivered by a designated agent."

Other states essentially permit voting to go on after the election. In New Jersey, ballots "must be received within 144 hours (six days) of the close of the polls if postmarked on or before Election Day. Mail-delivered ballots without postmarks that arrive within 48 hours of the close of the polls will be considered valid." Postmarked or not!

Postmarks are an iffy business these days anyway. The United States Postal System does not postmark most mail, though they will do so on request—go ahead and wait your turn in line at the post office!

In New York, thousands of ballots in the 2020 primary election showed up without a postmark. Federal Judge Analisa Torres ruled that "despite the Postal Service's best efforts, there is uncontroverted evidence that thousands of absentee ballots for the June 23 primary were not postmarked. This could be due to a number of human or mechanical errors." She decided that because "evidence showed that" invalidated ballots "were mailed on time," they should be counted.

California is another state that allows late ballots to be counted for a week after Election Day, though supposedly they require a postmark indicating they were mailed on time. In Pennsylvania, the law holds that ballots have to be received by Election Day to be counted, but a last-minute state supreme court ruling extended that limit by three days.

Pennsylvania also changed its rules on signature verification a few weeks before the 2020 election. The Democrat Secretary of State issued a guidance that "Pennsylvania Election Code does not authorize the county board of elections to set aside returned absentee or mail-in ballots based solely on signature analysis by the county board of elections."

Our election system has melted down into a nightmare scenario where millions of ballots could be mailed to addresses where a voter once lived. Campaign workers are paid to sniff around for blank ballots and encourage the holder to fill them out. These can be collected and brought to polling places, or dropped in the mail at some point around or after Election Day. They are opened and counted by temporary, lightly trained staffers who are counseled to go easy on matters such as who signed them or when they were mailed.

Republicans who have opposed the denigration of Election Day through ballot harvesting, early voting, and mail-in voting have been forced to swallow their opposition and compete for voters under these news rules. This political calculation may be understandable in the short term, but I worry if, in the long term, this will lead to the cementing of election rules that are fundamentally at odds with free and fair elections.

It's no wonder that people have legitimate questions about the conduct of American elections. And it's also no wonder that the powers that be are working overtime to make sure those questions don't get asked.

CHAPTER 6

THE BIG LIE

According to the mainstream media and the Biden regime currently running Washington, January 6, 2021, was the worst day in American history. President Joe Biden calls it the day "we nearly lost America—lost it all." The riot at the Capitol was, in the words of Representative Alexandria Ocasio-Cortez, "a terror attack" that left "almost 10 dead."

But that narrative, by and large, is wrong—the product of extreme Democrat gamesmanship working hand in glove with media more intent on advancing the party line than reporting the truth. Judicial Watch has uncovered some startling findings that show just how far partisan actors have distorted the truth to undermine civil liberties.

A month after the riot, House Speaker Nancy Pelosi established a special committee to "Investigate the January 6th Attack on the United States Capitol." The committee met for a year, interviewing one thousand witnesses, reviewing over one million documents, and watching hundreds of hours of video evidence. Her goal was to build a narrative, not to share the truth—and that was clear from the beginning.

The first week of the committee's hearings revolved around the testimony of police officers who were present during the riot, some of whom wept as they recounted the violence they encountered in pushing back against an angry mob of protesters. Caroline Edwards, a Capitol Police officer, described a scene out of a war. "There were officers on the ground. They were bleeding. They were throwing up," she said. "I saw friends with blood all over their faces. I was slipping in people's blood. I was catching people as they fell. It was carnage. It was chaos."

Michael Fanone, an officer with the DC Metropolitan Police Department, described how the mob "began to beat me, with their fists and with what felt like hard metal objects. . . . I was aware enough to recognize I was at risk of being stripped of, and killed with, my own firearm. I was electrocuted, again and again and again with a Taser. I'm sure I was screaming, but I don't think I could even hear my own voice." Fortunately, he explained, he appealed to the humanity of the mob by saying, "I've got kids." At that point, "some in the crowd stepped in and assisted me."[1]

Through the work of the January 6 Committee, the narrative of what happened on January 6 has focused sharply on the violence and death that attended what has been described as an effort to overthrow the government.

It quickly became apparent that "January 6" was being used by Left Democrats to damage the Trump brand, label his supporters as terrorists, and make verboten and criminal any questions about the 2020 election—and, of course, the 2024 election.

The Left pointed to several police officers whom they claimed had been killed by the mob. The death of Brian Sicknick, a Capitol Police officer who died the evening of January 7, was initially treated as a homicide brought on by being sprayed with pepper spray and beaten with a fire extinguisher by protestors. However, it was later determined that Sicknick—whose funeral urn lay in honor in the Capitol Rotunda—died of a stroke. Four officers took their own lives in the months following January 6, and some observers—typically January 6 maximalists like Kamala Harris or Alexandria Ocasio-Cortex—count them among the victims of the day's events.

Several people did die on January 6 at the Capitol. But they were all protesters. Kevin Greeson, a fifty-five-year-old Alabama man, had a heart attack and died on the grounds of the Capitol. Benjamin Phillips, a fifty-year-old Pennsylvanian computer programmer, suffered a stroke and died outside the Capitol, too. The *New York Times* originally reported that Roseanne Boyland, a thirty-four-year-old Georgia woman, had been crushed to death by a stampeding mob, but the medical examiner found that she in fact died of a drug overdose.

But only one individual was officially determined to be a homicide victim on January 6. That person was Ashli Babbitt, an Air Force veteran who was shot dead by Lieutenant Michael Byrd, a Capitol Police officer who was not in uniform. Ashli Babbitt was crawling through a broken window when she was killed. Her hands were visible. She was unarmed. She was putting no one in any danger, and there were no members of Congress anywhere around.

Lieutenant Byrd, Ashli's killer, did not identify himself as law enforcement to the crowd. He fired his gun without warning and was not in her line of sight. Ashli was effectively ambushed when she was shot in the left shoulder, dying soon after.

Her killer was never charged nor disciplined for killing an unarmed woman. In fact, he was promoted to captain and celebrated as a hero.

....

The events of January 6 were immensely complex, if you care to treat them as a vast criminal conspiracy worthy of millions of man-hours of investigation and the arrest and trial of over a thousand participants. From this point of view, the "insurrection" was a seditious and violent plan to overthrow the government, and everyone involved, however remotely, must be found and punished.

From another perspective, the January 6 riot at the Capitol was a mass protest that got out of hand, not unlike the hundreds of "peaceful protests" that rocked and burned the United States throughout the previous summer, causing billions of dollars of damage, injuries to thousands of police officers, and at least nineteen deaths. Thousands of rioters methodically set about attacking cops, burning buildings, and attacking federal buildings, yet very few people faced any serious charges.

There was certainly no effort to reconstruct the minute-by-minute efforts by an organized group of anarchists to destroy the federal courthouse in Portland over a series of months, and certainly no mass roundup of every participant in the siege. The FBI did not release footage of the attacks and "crowdsource" information regarding the identity of the rioters so they could be arrested and tried.

There are many major questions about January 6 that have gone unanswered, or even unasked. One important major question I have is, if the attack on the Capitol was a well-crafted insurrection, in which the seat of government was breached and rioters actually took over the Senate chambers, why did it end? What made it stop and caused the seditionists to leave? The police did not mount a counteroffensive to drive out the rebels. They seem to have looked around, stolen a few souvenirs, and left.

This is a basic and crucial question. If there was really a plan to stop the count of the votes of the Electoral College, what was it, and how were the insurrectionists going to install Trump as the president? Was there was really a plan, or was it, as it seemed at the time, an ugly, embarrassing debacle?

There are other questions. The police knew there was a plan to have a big "Stop the Steal" rally on the Ellipse, where President Trump would speak, followed by a march to the Capitol. We know, based on emails and other communications that Judicial Watch sued to get, that there were concerns about crowd control and security. Yet the Capitol was relatively unsecured.

Video from the day offers a variety of conflicting narratives that resist coherence. At some entrances the police blocked passage and demonstrators pushed violently to get inside; elsewhere, officers moved barriers out of the way and waved the marchers into the Capitol. Video from inside shows uniformed police escorting protestors around and offering directions, and there is ample documentation of supposed insurrectionists wandering around the Capitol rotunda respectfully admiring the statues and surroundings.

Was the Capitol riot on January 6 a good thing? Absolutely not. There was violence and lawlessness.

Was the Capitol riot a revolution or seditious conspiracy to topple the legitimate government? Absolutely not. It was a protest against an election tainted by obvious irregularities that devolved into an ugly scrap that spent itself within a few hours. The congressional investigation into the events of January 6 was not a fact-finding project along the lines of the 9/11 Commission. It was a partisan witch hunt with a predetermined conclusion that President Trump and his team had fomented a revolutionary mob to install him as dictator.

The January 6 Committee was originally supposed to be bicameral, but it couldn't get Senate approval. It was supposed to be bipartisan, but Speaker Nancy Pelosi refused to allow Congressmen Jim Jordan and Jim Banks—whose service would impair the "integrity of the investigation"—to sit on the committee. The Republican delegation refused to go along with Pelosi's unprecedented meddling with their choice of members, and so boycotted the committee entirely. Pelosi wound up appointing two strongly anti-Trump Republicans to the committee, which, as the *New York Times* approvingly noted a year later, held a series of hearings that offered "clear, uninterrupted narratives about President Donald J. Trump's effort to undercut the peaceful transfer of power."

But the January 6 Committee did delve into the many unanswered questions regarding the events leading up to and occurring on that day. Some of these questions have already been addressed in this book, such as: Was the 2020 election fair? Some of those questions will be addressed in this chapter, such as: Why was the Capitol undersecured that day? What was the objective, if any, of the rioters? And, vitally: Why was an unarmed woman called Ashli Babbitt, a veteran of active duty in the armed forces, shot and killed, and why didn't her killer face any consequences?

....

Judicial Watch began asking these questions immediately. On January 21, 2021, we sent a letter to the United States Capitol Police (USCP) requesting:

- Email communications between the US Capitol Police Executive Team and the Capitol Police Board concerning the security of the Capitol on January 6, 2021. The timeframe of this request is from January 1, 2021 through January 10, 2021
- Email communications of the Capitol Police Board with the Federal Bureau of Investigation, the US Department of Justice, and the US Department of Homeland Security concerning the security of the Capitol on January 6, 2021. The timeframe of this request is from January 1, 2021 through January 10, 2021
- All video footage from within the Capitol between 12:00 p.m. and 9:00 p.m. on January 6, 2021

We heard back from the USCP concerning our request three weeks later. James W. Joyce, the senior counsel of the USCP, let us know that, because Congress doesn't consider itself subject to Freedom of Information law, "We decline to provide the information requested in the attached January 21, 2021 Records Request. The email communications and video footage information requested in the attached are not public records."

Judicial Watch responded immediately by filing suit against the USCP in federal court. We argued that "the requested communications and video footage are public records because they were created or received by an agency of the legislative branch for the purpose of recording official actions. In addition, the requested communications and video footage are of legal significance."

I said at the time, "The public has a right to know about how Congress handled security and what all the videos show of the US Capitol riot. What are Nancy Pelosi and Chuck Schumer trying to hide from the American people?"

Quite a lot, as it turned out.

Judicial Watch next sued the Department of Defense for its failure to release all emails concerning "the deployment of US troops around the Capitol complex in Washington, DC, sent to and from Secretary of Defense Lloyd Austin, Deputy Secretary Kathleen H. Hicks, Joint Chiefs Chairman Gen. Mark A. Milley, and/or Vice Chairman Gen. John E. Hyten."

We also sued the Department of the Interior—which runs the United States Park Police—to make available records of all communications, "including emails and text messages," between the US Park Police and the DC Police, the FBI, the Capitol Police, and the Congressional Sergeants at Arms offices. We also asked to see "all intelligence reports, memoranda, updates, and warnings received by the US Park Police regarding the January 6, 2021, pro-Trump rally and/or protest at the Capitol Building."

The files we received show clearly that the Capitol Police were well aware of the fact that major protests were planned for January 6, the same day that the Congress would meet to certify the Electoral Votes. For instance, an email dated December 22, 2020, from the "Supervisory Special Agent" of the Intelligence Operations Section of the USCP, whose name was redacted, to the Assistant Commander of the Intelligence & Counterintelligence Branch of the Park Police, reads:

Good Morning,

I know we've been getting a lot of open source info from various individuals regarding protests on 1/6. This follows what we've been seeing, but we still wanted to put it on your radars. The Disqus comments were a pain to get to in the article, but eventually it worked for me.

It was well known among all the law enforcement agencies whose ambits overlapped in the Federal district in Washington that January 6 would see significant crowds. By December 30, according to a report from the Inspector General of the Department of Defense, twenty-three protest groups had registered to participate in or indicated that they planned to attend the rally on January 6. The total number of rally participants was estimated at about 25,000.[2]

The Sergeants at Arms offices were lackadaisical about the potential for trouble on the day of the protest. It's true they were busy, having to plan for the swearing in of the new Congress on January 3, and then preparing for the inauguration on January 20. But communications among the various agencies, and intraoffice memoranda, indicate that the USCP, under the direct control of the House Sergeant at Arms and thus then-speaker Nancy Pelosi, were stymied in their efforts to ensure a safe and secure Capitol.

In the days and weeks after January 6, Nancy Pelosi and other key regime leaders promoted the narrative that the riot at the Capitol was not just an attack on "Our Democracy," but completely unique in American history. Not only were the Capitol Police overwhelmed by the rioters, *but it couldn't have been avoided.* The "worst attack on the Capitol in two centuries," as the *New York Times* explained in a July 2021 article defending Nancy Pelosi's role, had nothing to do with the Speaker of the House, who, according to the *Times*, "is not responsible for the security of Congress. That is the job of the Capitol Police, an agency Ms. Pelosi only indirectly influences."

But the Speaker of the House appoints the House Sergeant at Arms, a role that is understood to be generally non-partisan yet fully answerable to the Speaker. Sergeant at Arms isn't like a federal judgeship, which is a lifetime appointment. The office of the Sergeant at Arms is a tool of the legislative body and answers to the head of that body.

In the leadup to January 6, the Sergeant at Arms resisted any military presence around the Capitol because of the "optics." On the morning of January 3, Steven Sund, chief of the USCP, asked the Sergeants at Arms of the Senate and the House of Representatives if he could submit an official request to have the DC National Guard (DCNG) support his crowd control efforts at the Capitol on January 6. But according to a Department of Defense report, "the Sergeants at Arms did not approve submitting a request asking DCNG for support. Mr. Sund added that the House Sergeant at Arms expressed concerns about the optics of National Guard members around the Capitol."

Nancy Pelosi evidently didn't want to make it look as though the military was facilitating an illegal coup. The essential demand of the rally on January 6 was for then–vice president Mike Pence, as the presiding officer of the Senate, to refuse to accept the votes of states that were constitutionally questionable. Congressman Jim Jordan wrote a text to Trump's Chief of Staff Mark Meadows on January 5, outlining the theory behind this suggestion.

On January 6, 2021, Vice President Mike Pence, as President of the Senate, should call out all electoral votes that he believes are unconstitutional as no electoral votes at all—in accordance with guidance from founding father Alexander Hamilton and judicial precedence. "No legislative act," wrote Alexander Hamilton in Federalist No. 78, "contrary to the Constitution, can be valid." The court in *Hubbard v. Lowe* reinforced this truth: "That an unconstitutional statute is not a law at all is a proposition no longer open to discussion." 226 F. 135, 137 (SDNY 1915), appeal dismissed, 242 U.S. 654 (1916). Following this rationale, an unconstitutionally appointed elector, like an unconstitutionally enacted statute, is no elector at all.[3]

Other advisors suggested a delay in the counting of the Electoral Votes until court challenges could be heard in states where the vote appeared illegitimate due to abnormalities in the count or illegal changes to the balloting process. While many of these arguments were controversial and novel, it is beyond argument that the 2020 election was irregular. So tensions were running high.

The Sergeant at Arms had plenty of reason to expect that the rally might get rowdy and require extra reinforcements. On November 14, 2020, eleven days after the election, thousands of supporters of President Trump rallied in Washington at Freedom Plaza. They were confronted by counterprotesters, including antifa activists in guerrilla-style black bloc gear. The two groups mostly screamed at each other, but after nightfall fights broke out, and there was at least one stabbing. Police arrested twenty people for offenses including firearm violations, assaulting a police officer, and disorderly conduct.

A month later, on December 12, thousands of Trump supporters again gathered at Freedom Plaza, and were again met by a counterprotest. As darkness fell antifa activists formed "bike walls" and engaged in fights with Trump supporters. Four people were stabbed and two dozen were arrested.

Of course, we don't have to limit ourselves to looking at 2020 election-related rallies that degenerated into mobs if we want to talk about political violence in DC. And we don't have to go back to the 1967 March on the Pentagon or the 1968 riots that killed thirteen people and wound up with martial law across the nation's capital. No, we can just look a few months before the 2020 election and see what happened when thousands of protesters tried to storm the White House after a career criminal and drug addict died during an arrest in Minnesota.

George Floyd died—was "murdered"—on May 25, 2020, in Minneapolis. He was passing a counterfeit twenty-dollar bill, and was apprehended in his car outside a grocery store. Ranting and raving and begging not to be shot, and complaining that he couldn't breathe in a police vehicle, Floyd was placed on the ground. The senior officer, Derek Chauvin, used his knee to restrain Floyd in a manner that by all accounts seems consistent with Minneapolis Police Department procedure.

But he died, probably at least in part from the massive quantities of drugs in his system. A civilian took a video of Officer Chauvin nonchalantly kneeling on what was reported as Floyd's neck, supposedly cutting off his air supply, but was actually his upper shoulder. The video went viral and America went totally mad. Probably in delayed reaction to the repression of the pandemic lockdown, and partly as a ginned-up effort by the Left to sow chaos and fear in advance of Trump's potential reelection, American liberals and radicals took to the streets to march, scream, riot, and burn.

In Washington, massive protests centering in Lafayette Square turned dangerous as rioters attempted to storm the gates of the White

House. The Secret Service downplayed the violence of the attacks. Agents, other federal law enforcement, and DC police were reportedly hit with rocks and pelted with urine; some suffered broken bones. None of them became famous, however, or were invited to testify to Congress about the trauma they suffered. In fact, tens of thousands of law enforcement officers were injured in the summer of 2020, and there was no effort made by the media or other regime partners to exalt their suffering.

The claim that "protectees" were never in danger is belied by the fact that President Trump and his family were moved to a secure bunker after protesters breached fences that had been erected to expand the barrier around the White House.

What's curious is that the national media loved the idea that Trump was "hiding" or "cowering" in a secure bunker "as protests raged," as PBS put it. Supposed political satirist Stephen Colbert compared Trump to Hitler, noting: "Well, if history has taught us anything it's that things always work well for strongmen who retreat to underground bunkers."

All good fun. But six months later, when the riot at the Capitol happened, no one in the mainstream media cracked a smile when Representative Alexandria Ocasio-Cortez claimed that her life was in danger on January 6 as the result of a "very close encounter," even though she was in an office building nowhere near the rioters.[4] When Senator Patty Murray told Judy Woodruff on *PBS NewsHour* on February 12 that she heard "explosions . . . loud explosions" in a Capitol hallway, nobody asked her to clarify what she was talking about, since there have been no other reports of any explosions from that day.

We shouldn't forget the rest of the drama that plagued DC at the start of the "Summer of Floyd." A historic church across the street from the White House, St. John's Episcopal Church, was set on fire and sustained major damage to its basement; the church was also defaced with antifa graffiti. The headquarters of the AFL-CIO was broken into by a violent mob, which smashed windows and set the lobby on fire.

Dozens of stores in Washington were looted. Monuments were defaced and several statues were torn down. Order was restored when President Trump ordered some 6,000 federal troops from disparate agencies including the National Guard, FBI, Secret Service, US Marshals Service, and others.

The point being that, only six months later, the local security and political infrastructure could have considered the idea that a big rally might get out of hand, and they had the recent experience and know-how to contain it.

Judicial Watch demanded, and in October 2023 finally received (through our lawsuit), the details about communications relating to preparations for the January 6 rally from James W. Joyce, senior counsel in the Office of the General Counsel for the Capitol Police. Joyce describes emails among senior officials of the United States Capitol Police (USCP) in January 2021 that show warnings of possible January 6 protests that could lead to serious disruptions at the US Capitol. These new documents shed important light on the extent to which high-level security staff were aware of the problem.

Our original request in 2021 was denied by the Capitol Police on the grounds that Congress is not subject to common law provision that gives public the right to access government information and, even if the public did have a right to those public records, the documents we wanted were not technically public records. Eventually we prevailed, and James W. Joyce revealed the existence of the following emails:

A January 3, 2021, email, with attachment, from the USCP Deputy Chief to a Board member and others at USCP and in Congress providing a detailed "special event assessment" of anticipated protest activity in advance of the January 6,

2021 Joint Session of Congress. The attached document is marked on each page "For Official Use Only/Law Enforcement Sensitive."

A January 5, 2021, email, with map attachment, from the USCP Chief to two Board members detailing a proposed "bike rack" security perimeter for January 6, 2021, and proposing further discussion.

A January 5, 2021, email, with map attachment, from the USCP Chief to two Board members detailing a proposed security perimeter for January 6, 2021.

A January 5, 2021, email, with social media post and map attachments, from the USCP Deputy Chief to a Board member and others at USCP and in Congress reporting "a significant uptick in new visitors" to a "historical website" containing information on Capitol system tunnels. The Deputy Chief describes proposed attempts by unauthorized individuals to block members of Congress from entering the Capitol building, through tunnels or otherwise.

A January 5, 2021, email from the USCP Deputy Chief to a Board member and others at USCP and in Congress alerting them to an online website soliciting information on high-level government officials and their expected whereabouts on January 6, 2021, and linking to the website's article entitled *Why the Second American Revolution Starts Jan 6*.

A January 6, 2021, email from the USCP Chief to Board members and others at USCP and in Congress relaying that the President had completed a speech at the Ellipse and that a large group was preparing to approach the Capitol.

A January 6, 2021, email thread between the USCP Chief, two Board members, and congressional staffers responding to questions on the status of evacuations and relocations of certain buildings on the Capitol Grounds on January 6, 2021, and relaying information on crowds gathering near the Washington Monument and on Capitol Grounds on January 6, 2021.

A series of four January 6, 2021, emails from the USCP Deputy Chief to a Board member and others at the USCP and in Congress providing four updates throughout the course of January 6, 2021. These updates contain intelligence assessments, information on arrests, coordination with other law enforcement agencies, crowd estimates, scheduling of high-level government officials, threat and incident reports, medical responses, and officer deployment status.

A January 7, 2021, email, with photo attachment, from the USCP Deputy Chief to Board member and others in Congress providing an update on the arrest and subsequent charging of an armed individual found in a "suspicious vehicle" on January 6, 2021.

So the Capitol Police were aware, before January 6, that people were trying to figure out the tunnel system underneath the Capitol, and were soliciting information on the expected whereabouts of elected officials. But for reasons of "optics," the Capitol Police were ordered, essentially, to stand down.[5]

Republican House representatives, some of whom were blocked by Speaker Pelosi from serving on her special committee, conducted their own investigation into "Security Failures at the United States Capitol on January 6, 2021." Their report, though overlooked by the national media, reveals a slate of facts that support the thesis that Nancy Pelosi and her operatives in the office of the Sergeant at Arms and, by extension, the Capitol Police, did not want to defend the Capitol at a moment when they knew that there was danger of a riot.

"Even if every USCP officer had been at work that day," the Republican report contends, "their numbers would still have been insufficient to hold off the rioters due to a lack of training and equipment. The USCP was set up to fail, and there have been scant signs of progress toward addressing these weaknesses." The report cites an analysis of the day's events conducted by the USPC Office of the Inspector General—a report that is not available in an unredacted form to the public—which is damning in regard to how the Capitol Police were hamstrung in their efforts to secure the Capitol in advance of the January 6 rally.[6]

Was the weak defense of the Capitol merely a question of "optics"? Did Nancy Pelosi worry that the presence of too many armed security agents would make it look like she was trying to force through the count of the votes of the Electoral College undemocratically? Or did she—as some have suggested—set the USCP up to fail, because she wanted a different sort of optics: the optics of right-wing mass violence, to erase the already fading memory of the Summer of Floyd, and establish the basis for a new political regime based around the promise of "Defending Our Democracy"?

....

It could be a mixture of the two, or perhaps both. No one really knows what Nancy Pelosi thought or hoped might happen if angry rioters—perhaps stirred up by *agents provocateurs* who never faced legal consequences equal to their apparent role in the disturbance—breached the Capitol.

But we do know one thing for certain about January 6, which is that one person, and only person, was a homicide victim that day. And she was shot dead by a police officer whose application of the rules of engagement regarding use of force was loose at best.

The murder—and I will call it that—of Ashli Babbitt happened at 2:44 pm on January 6. Almost three years to the day after her death

Judicial Watch filed a $30 million wrongful death lawsuit against the US government on behalf of her family.

As the lawsuit details:

> Ashli loved her country and wanted to show her support for President Trump's America First policies and to see and hear the president speak live while he remained in office. Ashli did not go to Washington as part of a group or for any unlawful or nefarious purpose. She was there to exercise what she believed were her God-given, American liberties and freedoms.
>
> Ashli Babbitt had previously entered the Capitol, on the Senate side, and was then directed by an officer to go around the building to the House side. That is scarcely mentioned in coverage of her murder. But it speaks to the bizarre and unresolved way in which that day's events unfolded. Yes, in certain instances mobs threw aside barriers or dramatically and unnecessarily climbed up parts of the building; but there is also video evidence of officers opening up barriers and waving protesters in. In some cases rioters were shoving and hitting police officers, but in other cases they can be seen chatting amiably with each other inside the Capitol.[7]

Judicial Watch has been in the forefront of suing to get all the video of the day released to the public, so the people have the opportunity to see what was going on with their own eyes, and come to an informed conclusion about the rally that turned into a riot and that petered out as the rebels left to have dinner.

But the narrative that Nancy Pelosi and the national media chose to run with was a one-dimensional justification for their seizure of state power in the name of Their Democracy, which means, essentially, promoting a grotesque, unpopular agenda of open borders, racial resentment, centralization of power, and imprisoning their enemies. And as part of their narrative, what happened to Ashli Babbitt is beneath comment. And I mean that almost literally. In the entire 845 page Final Report of the Select Committee to Investigate the January 6 Attack on the United States Capitol Ashli Babbitt's name comes up seven times—seven—and then just in passing. One would think that a massive investigation into the facts of the matter of a "deadly assault" would at least consider the facts of the one indisputable homicide that took place that day. But the point of the investigation was never to find facts—it was simply to connect the day's rioting directly to the words of Donald Trump in such a way that the regime could find a way to jail him.

The Judicial Watch wrongful death lawsuit continues:

> The shooting occurred at the east entrance to the Speaker's Lobby. After demonstrators filled the hallway outside the lobby, two individuals in the crowded, tightly packed hallway struck and dislodged the glass panels in the lobby doors and the right door sidelight.
>
> Lt. Byrd, who is a USCP commander and was the incident commander for the House on January 6, 2021, shot Ashli on sight as she raised herself up into the opening of the right door sidelight. Lt. Byrd later confessed that he shot Ashli before seeing her hands or assessing her intentions or even identifying her as female. Ashli was unarmed. Her hands were up in the air, empty, and in plain view of Lt. Byrd and other officers in the lobby. Ashli posed no threat to the safety of anyone. Not one member of Congress was in the lobby, which was guarded by multiple armed police officers. Additional armed police officers were in the hallway outside the lobby and/or on the adjoining stairway.

Ashli could not have seen Lt. Byrd, who was positioned far to Ashli's left and on the opposite side of the doors, near an opening to the Retiring Room, a distance of approximately 15 feet and an angle of approximately 160 degrees. Sgt. Timothy Lively, one of the armed officers guarding the lobby doors from the hallway, later told officials investigating the shooting, "I saw him . . . there was no way that woman would've seen that."

Lt. Byrd, who was not in uniform, did not identify himself as a police officer or otherwise make his presence known to Ashli. Lt. Byrd did not give Ashli any warnings or commands before shooting her dead.

There was virtually no effort by the federal government to investigate the shooting death of Ashli Babbitt. The Department of Justice routinely looks into controversial police-related deaths to determine if the federal courts need to step in. When they do, they commit significant time and resources to their investigations. In 2014, after Mike Brown was shot dead by Ferguson, Missouri, officer Darren Wilson, the FBI sent forty agents to gather evidence, and the Department of Justice assigned multiple attorneys to consider charging Wilson with a crime. They took eight months to finally announce that there was no case to be made.

In the case of Eric Garner, a 400-pound man who died of cardiac arrest while resisting arrest in Staten Island, the Department of Justice took five years to investigate the case before concluding there was nothing there. Derrick Chauvin, who was convicted by a state court of murdering George Floyd and sentenced to 250 months in prison, was then indicted by a federal court and wound up pleading guilty to charges of depriving Floyd of his civil rights. He received a twenty-one-year sentence, to be served concurrently. His fellow officers were also charged with federal civil rights charges and received lesser, though still stiff, prison sentences.

In the case of Ashli Babbitt's murder, the government not only concluded its investigation of the killing in mid-April, determining that "the US Attorney's Office for the District of Columbia and the Civil Rights Division of the US Department of Justice will not pursue criminal charges against the US Capitol Police officer involved in the fatal shooting of 35-year-old Ashli Babbitt," they withheld the name of the officer who shot her.

It might make sense to keep the names of the SEAL Team Six a secret. And in countries like Mexico special police officers often work in anonymity because of fears of assassination. But in America there is no justification for sealing the name of a police officer involved in shooting a civilian.

Michael Byrd came forward of his own accord to reveal his identity in August 2021, a few days after the DC police department announced that he would not face disciplinary charges for shooting an unarmed woman. Byrd went on the *NBC Nightly News with Lester Holt* to complain about "vicious and cruel" things that were said about him, and to explain that he "showed the utmost courage on January 6."

We at Judicial Watch were amazed to discover early in 2023 that the government let Byrd and his pet stay, at taxpayers' expense, in a special "Distinguished Visitor Suite" at Joint Base Andrews, from July 8, 2021, through January 28, 2022, at a rate of about a thousand bucks a week. The US Capitol Police—which was not the police force for which Byrd worked—paid his bill every ten days.

"These extraordinary revelations forced out by a Judicial Watch FOIA lawsuit show Defense Department facilities were used to provide long-term housing for the Capitol Hill police officer who shot and killed Air Force veteran Ashli Babbitt," I said at the time.[8]

It's not like Michael Byrd was a great cop, either. Our wrongful death lawsuit details how based on prior incidents involving Lt. Byrd, the Capitol Police, Capitol Police Board, and ultimately Congress, as Lt. Byrd's employer, "knew or should have known that Lt. Byrd was prone to behave in a dangerous or otherwise incompetent manner." As the lawsuit explains:

Less than two years before January 6, 2021, on or about February 25, 2019, Lt. Byrd left his loaded Glock 22—the same firearm he used to shoot and kill Ashli Babbitt—in a bathroom in the Capitol Visitor Center (CVC) complex. Lt. Byrd's loaded Glock was discovered during a routine security sweep later the same day. Approximately 15,000 to 20,000 people pass through the CVC, which serves as the main entrance for visitors to the US Capitol, daily during peak season (March-July). Lawmakers and staff charged with oversight of the USCP were not made aware of the incident until contacted by a reporter.

Lt. Byrd's police powers had been revoked on more than one occasion prior to January 6, 2021, for failing to meet or complete semiannual firearms qualification requirements. In fact, Lt. Byrd had a reputation among peers for not being a good shot. Under USCP's range management system, an officer who fails to meet firearm qualification requirements is given one week of remedial training. If the officer still fails to qualify after remedial training, police powers are then revoked until the officer qualifies.

Lt. Byrd's police powers also were revoked for a prior off-duty shooting into a stolen, moving vehicle in which the occupants were teenagers or juveniles. The stolen vehicle was Lt. Byrd's car. Lt. Byrd fired multiple shots at the fleeing vehicle in a suburban area. Stray bullets from Lt. Byrd's firearm struck the sides of homes nearby. An official investigation found that Lt. Byrd's use of force was not justified.

Michael Byrd is no hero. He is an out-of-control cop with an itchy trigger finger. The record shows he left his gun in a bathroom in a busy visitor center. He can't shoot straight. And he fired his gun impetuously in a residential area because some kids stole his car.

In a just system, Ashli Babbitt would be mourned as a victim of true police malfeasance, and Michael Byrd would have faced a significant criminal investigation. But America has entered a netherworld of justice and reason, where the Left can turn scoundrels into heroes and innocent murdered women into traitors.

As our lawsuit for her family notes:

The facts speak truth. Ashli was ambushed when she was shot by Lt. Byrd. Multiple witnesses at the scene yelled, "you just murdered her."

CHAPTER 7

BALLOONS, DOGS, AND A MYSTERIOUS DISAPPEARANCE

Judicial Watch is a serious civil rights organization. We sue the government to release information that is of vital importance to a functioning democracy. We hold power to account. This book has addressed major crises in American life: the pandemic, electoral fraud, top-level political corruption, and the weaponization of venerable institutions for authoritarian ends.

But sometimes we uncover minor scandals and happenings that may not necessarily strike at the heart of a constitutional republic, but which are nevertheless highly embarrassing to the powers that rule over us. Judicial Watch thinks it's worthwhile to highlight these bagatelles, first of all because they are a little bit insane and interesting, and second because they cast a telling light on the everyday corruption and abuse of our government.

Foreign affairs are always a power game, and the purpose of diplomacy is to put a pretty face on ferocious jockeying for position. America's dealings with China are especially tied up with the appearance of having the upper hand, or "face." Having "face" in Chinese means maintaining social reputation, dignity, and honor. Losing "face" equals shame, embarrassment, and loss of respect.

The Trump years were tough on China. Donald Trump was fond of presenting strength, and he put the Chinese on the back foot regarding trade and Taiwan. Immediately after Biden took over, though, the Chinese Communist Party took a more aggressive stance on issues that sound mostly symbolic. But in the world of international diplomacy, symbols, language, and tone are as meaningful as troop movements or the massing of battleships in war.

In March 2021, the Biden White House invited Chinese officials to a meeting in Alaska, in an effort to set a cordial tone between the two nations and get bilateral relations off to a good start. Instead, Chinese Foreign Minister Wang Yi and Yang Jiechi, director of the Central Foreign Affairs Commission of the Chinese Communist Party, openly mocked Secretary of State Anthony Blinken, subjecting the American side to a lengthy harangue.

Yang dismissed Blinken's commitment to the "rules-based international order" as a screen for American dominance and an excuse to impose regime change on other counties. He said that American democracy is a sham, and that the Black Lives Matter movement shows the United States is in no position to lecture China about human rights. The Chinese officials ridiculed America's world posture and its supposed championing of democratic values.

Blinken offered some lame responses, but the meeting was widely understood as China flexing its muscle before weak American leadership.

In February 2023, sharp-eyed airline passengers spotted a massive balloon floating over Montana. Soon, observers on the ground began tracking the aircraft, which was eventually identified as a Chinese surveillance balloon. The sphere, about 150 feet in diameter, floated across US airspace, presumably intercepting signals intelligence or taking pictures. It was eventually shot down off the coast of South Carolina.

Analysts agreed that the Chinese wanted the balloon to be noticed, and that its purpose was to embarrass the US government while brazenly collecting intelligence. They succeeded. For a week the nation watched as its government dithered, alternately insisting that the balloon was "not a major breach," and denouncing it as a violation of American sovereignty. After it was shot down, China demanded the return of the equipment tethered to the balloon.

China continued to rub America's nose in its disrespect. When Blinken visited China in June 2023, he was met by a low-level official, and there was no red carpet laid out to welcome him. Blinken spent two days talking with underlings before he was granted a meeting with Premier Xi. The official picture of their meeting shows Xi at the head of a grand table, with Blinken sitting to the side.

But the weirdest and most humiliating gesture of disrespect from the Chinese emerged in the first few weeks of the Biden administration, right after Beijing announced the latest weapon in its Covid-19 arsenal: anal swabs.

You may have forgotten, but there was a period in 2021 when everyone was testing, testing, testing. Cotton swabs, little vials, and testing sticks were the national obsession, and we all breathed deep signs of relief when we were negative, or settled in for weeks of government-endorsed "quarantine" if we tested positive. The hype in those days was so tweaked up, you may recall, that there were instructions for us to get undressed at our front door and scrupulously wash our Amazon delivery boxes lest we contaminate our interiors.

In January 2021 the Chinese revealed that their labs—not the same ones that brought us the Covid virus, but maybe close—had pioneered the most effective Covid tests so far. A long cotton swab could be inserted a few inches into the anus, swirled about a few times, and then deliver the most accurate Covid results possible.

This became fodder for late-night jokes, but news reports emerged that the Chinese government had forced American diplomats entering their country to undergo anal swabbing.

These claims were quickly brushed under the carpet; the State Department indicated that such tests were "never agreed to," and said that "We have received assurances from MFA (Ministry of Foreign Affairs) that this testing was conducted in error and that diplomatic personnel are exempt from this requirement. Our guidance to diplomatic personnel remains the same as it has always been: to decline this test if it is asked of them."

The official Chinese response was that it never happened. "I checked this with my colleagues. As far as I know, China has never asked US diplomats stationed in China to do anal swab tests," said Chinese Foreign Ministry spokesperson Zhao Lijian.

Judicial Watch wasn't satisfied and decided to dig further. It is incomprehensible to imagine US diplomatic personnel being subjected to such a weird and degrading procedure when nasal or buccal swabs are readily available. In August 2021, after getting the runaround, we filed a FOIA lawsuit to obtain "All records about US diplomatic personnel in or seeking to enter China being subjected to anal swab tests for the Covid-19 virus, including all complaints and communications regarding such testing. This request does not seek any personal identifying information of US diplomatic personnel that may have been subjected to such testing."

We weren't looking to subject any American staff to any more embarrassment than they had already received. "Our diplomatic personnel were abused in a reprehensible way by the Chinese and the Biden administration seems to have done little in response—except to cover it up," I said at the time.[1]

In December 2021 we received eight pages of emails from the State Department regarding anal swabbing that indicated that at least two people had been subjected to the gross treatment. On January 25, 2021, an unidentified general services officer in the US Embassy, Beijing, sent emails to personnel evidently under quarantine after traveling to China under the subject line "Testing Guidance:"

Sorry for the strange questions, but I was directed by embassy management to survey our people and ensure we are not being asked to participate in the more invasive testing procedures.

The sender also writes:

There's no good way to ask this, but has any health authority asked you or your spouse to conduct an anal swab test? The embassy obviously does not authorize or permit this type of testing on diplomats, but others have been asked so I need to verify everyone's experience.

The testers may also ask to do an "environmental test" where they enter the residence and swab drinking glasses, furniture, etc. This is also not permitted. They may swab the **outside** of the doorknob, but nothing internal. [Emphasis in the original.]

For the record, our agreement is for nasal and/or throat swabs only. If you are asked to undergo either of the above or any other that seems inappropriate, please refuse and contact us immediately. We will escalate to [China's] MFA/FAO [foreign area officer] and go from there.

At 10:34 p.m. on January 26, 2021, one unidentified sender emailed an unidentified recipient under the subject line "Test:"

[Redacted] please call me at your convenient time [redacted]. Below text message came from [redacted]. This is not good!

At 10:39, the recipient responds:

This is becoming so non diplomatic status testing. Disgusting. I hope the GSO [general services officer] and VIP Beijing visits can do something about this. I am so disgusted right now.

The sender responds at 11:49 a.m. the next day: "At this point, if they will insist the anal test, we would like to just go back to the States."

Another recipient of the original "Testing Guidance" email responds on January 26:

> Thanks. I am hoping for a smooth covid test and release on Friday.

On January 26, an unidentified sender responds to the original "Test Guidance" email with a request for help:

> That is indeed a very strange test and first time we've heard as well.
>
> Fortunately, the tests we had at the Shanghai airports was just nose swab and one at Shanghai hotel on our 14th day was just throat swab.
>
> Do you have a good number we can call that we will definitely get a response right away once they come in for the test on Friday, January 29th? Last Friday, I tried to call 9 to 10 a.m. to be connected to anyone in the VIP visits and no one answered the office number and the mobile number same thing when we got inside the LMQC unit at 2:30 I started calling to inquire more guidelines and I was not able to talk to anyone.
>
> On January 27, another recipient of the "Test Guidance" email notifies his "team:"
>
> Team—FYI. [Redacted] being asked for anal swab and environmental test. Can Housing contact [redacted]? I'll have VIP contact FAO ASAP.

On March 4, a redacted sender emails a redacted recipient in the State Department's VIP Visits Section under the subject line "Swabs, swabs, and more swabs" (citing a Reuters article):

I hadn't heard this rule before:

"Travelers flying into Shanghai must undertake a full battery of tests including anal swabs, if more than five people on their airplane test positive for the virus, state media reported, citing one of the local CDC staff."

In response to this email, the recipient appears to email another person in the VIP Visits section about the new Chinese rule:

This is certainly different and a variation on the "close contact" rule.
VIP—please check with FAO again on this. Seems to be a CDC rule and given our history with close contacts and following hotel separations, want to make sure the MFA/FAO understand this is not acceptable for our people regardless of the reason.

On March 5, the VIP Visits sender emails the apparently same recipient:

Just checked with my contact from the PEK [Beijing International Capital Airport] customs. Airport only does nasal swab and throat swab. According to some Chinese social media, international travelers are required to get anal tests during centralized quarantine. It could happen on Day 3, Day 7, Day 14 or Day 21. Some people were tested once and some were twice. Samples were collected by medical staff or travelers themselves or from a fecal sample.

The recipient responds:

Thanks [redacted]. Interesting that there's no central policy on this given all the media attention and spin. Please keep me undated [sic] if anything changes.[2]

So far as this information went, it didn't seem like there had been much reported in the way of anal swabbing. But we hadn't gotten everything yet. Often times, agencies will respond to FOIA requests in dribs and drabs, burying the more important material in a second or third tranche of documents, perhaps hoping that the requester will have read through the first batch and grown bored.

Not Judicial Watch. We pride ourselves on reading every line and "turning every page" in the words of historian Robert Caro. In late January 2022 we received eleven pages of records from the US Department of State revealing that US diplomatic officials in China objected to being asked to submit to anal swab Covid testing by the Chinese government. The redacted documents show that at least one US employee was given an anal swab test for Covid "at his apartment."

On January 22, 2021—two days into the new Biden administration—a redacted general services officer from the US Consulate General in Shenyang sent an email with the subject "New Testing Method?":

So, a colleague from [redacted] telling our group [redacted] that he was given an anal COVID swab at his apartment. Just a heads up, as I am sure it is going to blow up soon . . . if you aren't already dealing with it. Employee's name is [redacted]. Just getting ahead before the word of mouth starts spreading.

A redacted official responds:

In what city did this occur? And what number test? And did he say if they gave any notice beforehand the test would be conducted in this manner? And was he presented with options.

A redacted official responds:

-Beijing
   -He is in his apartment as part of the +7 (from my understanding)
   -No notice or options as I can tell
   -He had to do both a nose and anal swab

Also on January 22, 2021, a management officer in the US Consulate in Shenyang, whose name is redacted, sent an email with the subject "RE: No Anal swabs for diplomats."

FAO [foreign area office] is telling the Embassy that it was a mistake to ask for anal swabs and that it didn't apply to diplomats. TBD how [redacted] will play it, but for now we'll have to tell people they don't have to do it. Reportedly you do it yourself in private so not as bad as I envisioned.

In a January 26, 2021, email regarding the anal COVID tests, a redacted U.S. official wrote:

I hope the GSO [general services office] and VIP Beijing visits can do something about this.

In a January 27, 2021, email labeled with the subject line "COVID TEST 21st DAY Hedeliza and Efren Balisi" is marked "Importance: High," a redacted US official wrote:

Team – FYI, [redacted] being asked for anal swab and environmental test. Can Housing contact [redacted]. I'll have VIP contact FAO ASAP.

A redacted official writes on January 27, 2021:

I have asked [redacted] to contact [redacted] immediately regarding the anal swab and environmental testing. He is calling them now.

A redacted official on January 27, 2021, responds:

Please contact the [redacted]. [Redacted] turned off the anal swab, and indicated that we are fine with and oral or nasal swab. He also turned off the inside the apartment environmental testing as I protested both of those items.

On May 5, 2021, a redacted official writes to Beijingvipvisits@state .gov with the subject line "Beijing PCS Arrival and Quarantine Questions:"

Hi. [Redacted] I'm planning to arrive in country in early August. What do we need to be aware of for planning purposes? Are we able to fly into Beijing directly? Someone mentioned that we have to fly into another city. We currently have reservations for Beijing, so we wanted to check before having the tickets issued.

We've been hearing a lot of horror stories about the quarantine in China. Unfortunately, the monthly newcomers call [redacted] land the calls aren't recorded, so we can't even hear the answers to others questions via a recording of the calls. So I hope you don't mind us asking our questions to you directly. We've had some conversations with the CLO and their office referred us to you for more specifics.

We have been talking with a number of [redacted] in China or those that recently left. We've heard a lot of horror stories about the quarantine upon arrival. We've heard about older children being separate from families during the quarantine, anal swab testing and real violations of diplomatic norms. Others have reported they were crammed in rooms with inadequate bedding—i.e. two twin beds for a family of four—and sub-par conditions bordering on detention center level living. It seems like diplomats and their families are not being treated according to acceptable norms. The escalation of the PRC's violations of diplomatic protections seems particularly concerning . . . .

A redacted official responds:

Anal swabs and "environmental testing" inside USG residences are not permitted for diplomatic staff. This acknowledgement of diplomatic rights has been confirmed repeatedly by MFA and FAO. If there is an attempt to conduct such a test, the traveler is fully within their rights to refuse testing and contact the Embassy.

Please note that the PRC travel, quarantine, hotel, and testing policies can and do change regularly with no warning and immediate effect. The guidance above is designed to give you an idea of the current landscape, but this is always subject to change as we've seen many times before. Please remain in contact with the Beijing VIP team on the latest guidance and we look forward to welcoming you and your family to Beijing in the future.

So an American diplomat to China was accosted in his apartment in Beijing and forced to undergo an anal swab for Covid, in addition to a nasal test. This ought to have been grounds for a major scandal. The principle of diplomatic immunity is ancient, almost primal. A diplomat traditionally was a stand-in for the body of the king; in today's terms a diplomat is a living representation of the state he was sent from. As such diplomats are treated with a high level of respect and deference.[3]

When the Chinese subjected an American diplomat to a degrading anal swab a few days after Joe Biden's inauguration, they were not-so-subtly sending a message to the new administration about how much respect they held for them, and for America generally. This should have prompted an immediate and furious response from Washington. But Biden, like Obama, operates with a public attitude of deference to abusive foreign regimes.

And so we lose face, bending over for our adversaries as the administration tries to hide the humiliations they allow our diplomats to suffer from the public. That's not a recipe for success, and invites aggression, as we now see across the world.

....

The night of July 18, 1969, destroyed the political aspirations of the youngest son and last great hope of the Kennedy family. Senator Ted Kennedy, accompanied by a young woman who had been his brother Robert's secretary, drove off a bridge on the east end of Chappaquiddick, an island off the east end of Martha's Vineyard, a popular vacation spot for Northeast elites. The senator got away fine; the woman in the car with him, Mary Jo Kopechne, drowned. Kennedy's actions before and after the crash have never been clarified, and the whole episode was covered up as quickly as possible.

Fifty-four years later, almost to the day, another odd, politically connected drowning death occurred just a mile or two from the site of Ted Kennedy's strange and fatal car crash, in the backyard of local resident and former president Barack Obama. On July 23, 2023, a paddleboarder in the Edgartown Great Pond drowned, evidently after falling in the brackish coastal pond. The victim, Tafari Campbell, was the Obama family's personal chef, having met the former president when he worked in the White House as a sous chef.

Judicial Watch filed a FOIA request to obtain the police report regarding Campbell's death. The report showed for the first time the involvement of the Secret Service in the emergency. The Secret Service reported him missing and that the body was found using sonar. The records also reported that clothing was found separate from the body and that he was not wearing a life vest. Several other important details were redacted regarding the July 23, 2023, drowning on Martha's Vineyard.

The records, released on August 23, 2023, include a July 23 CAD (computer aided dispatch) Incident Report:

Secret Service Agent [redacted] adv swimmers unable to locate the party at this time. Party last scene [*sic*] wearing all black, on a paddle board, African American male.

Rec'vd a 911 call from the above noted RP [reporting person] who identified as a Secret Service member. RP is req [requesting] at least an ambulance response, unsure of the exact services needed.

RP advd best access is from the residence, they are deploying a rescue swimmer and a zodiac boat right now.

RP adv no lifevest was worn, they have recovered the paddle board and clothing. Still no contact with missing party. They still have a boat and rescue swimmers in the area.

At 8:25 p.m., the report noted that the Oak Bluffs Fire Department was sending a dive team. At 8:36 p.m., a Coast guard helicopter was deployed, as was a state police helicopter.

In the reports sent by Police Chief Bruce McNamee, the names of a witness and a Secret Service agent are removed. In his email transmitting the reports, McNamee writes: "Per the request of the Ma State Police, the names of the witness and USSS agent have been redacted."

The police and fire departments made their base of operations at Wilson's Landing, a popular boat launch. Search and dive teams from Oak Bluffs, Tisbury, and West Tisbury joined the search.

The next day, Sgt. William Bishop wrote:

Once on location [Wilson's Landing] we established a command post. I requested through MSP a search helicopter, and Chief Schaeffer requested a USCG helicopter as well. Search & Dive teams from Edgartown, Oak Bluffs, Tisbury, West Tisbury responded via mutual aid. An extensive search began for several hours. A last known location was established, and Trooper Shaw of MSP also assisted with operations.

I instructed Officer Guest and Officer Dacey to commence a shoreline search effort starting from the closest house and working outward. Both Officers checked every house with waterfront access in the search area. Unfortunately, the search did not yield and results.

Both air wings conducted a search until their fuel supply forced a return to base.

At or about 11PM the dive and land search was suspended. Edgartown and Oak Bluffs Fire planned to continue a grid search by boat for the remainder of the night. At first light, dive team operations will continue. During the duration of this incident the entrance to Wilson's Landing was closed as to give responders room to work.

The next morning the dive team search continued, and a deceased Mr. Campbell was located using sonar. The investigation will now be handled by Massachusetts State Police and The Cape and Islands District Attorney's Office. No further action.[4]

"It is concerning that Judicial Watch had to push and push for information on this tragic death, such as the new revelation that the

Obamas' Secret Service protection reported Mr. Campbell missing," I remarked at the time. But a further wrinkle was added to the story in October 2023, when Judicial Watch received an additional forty pages of records from the Massachusetts State Police that indicate the presence of Barack Obama for a witness interview in the death investigation Mr. Campbell.

The records, which are heavily redacted, indicate Barack Obama arrived at the emergency response scene via motorcade. A short time later, a cold, wet woman, who was a witness, arrived. The next morning, the eyewitness was interviewed in the Obama residence, seemingly with Barack Obama again present. The records also detail the existence of a Secret Service video of Campbell and his paddleboarding companion entering the water, and the Secret Service emergency response in the immediate aftermath of the drowning. The state police records show they concluded "no foul play" in Campbell's "accidental" death.

The documents were produced to Judicial Watch in response to a July 25, 2003, Massachusetts Public Records Law request for all records relating to the death of Campbell.

The documents show Campbell's family told police that he had taken swimming lessons in 2019 but described his ability as "not a great swimmer." The drowning occurred in Edgartown Great Pond, which Massachusetts Environmental Police estimated "to be approximately seven to eight feet deep."

The records also show a female eyewitness, an Obama employee whose name is redacted, told state police that she saw Campbell "fall off his paddleboard, began splashing and became extremely panicked, yelling for help and subsequently went underwater very quickly." By the time she reached his paddleboard, the witness said Campbell had "disappeared into the extremely murky" water.

The records include a July 24, 2023, homicide/death report written by Mass. State Trooper Dustin Shaw that lists the details of the investigation into Campbell's death. In the narrative portion Shaw writes:

> The following is a summary of my observations of the video footage provided to me from this specific vantage point and is not intended to be an exact depiction of the overall entirety of the surveillance footage from [redacted] On Sunday, July 23, 2023, at approximately:

- 6:54 PM; two (2) individuals identified as CAMPBELL and [redacted] are observed walking on the boardwalk from the area of the residence, toward the shoreline of Edgartown Great Pond. Both CAMPBELL'S and [redacted] appearance and clothing are consistent with prior descriptions. Once near the shoreline, it appears that CAMPBELL and [redacted] obtain paddleboards and paddles from a small alcove near the shoreline, and subsequently enter the water.
- 7:40 PM; Secret Service Agent [redacted] (Rescue Swimmer) is observed running from his assigned post towards the shoreline of Edgartown Great Pond, utilizing his handheld radio.
- 7:42 PM; Agent [redacted] observed running from the shoreline of Edgartown Great Pond, towards the area of the Command Post.
- 7:43 PM; Agent [redacted] observed running back to shoreline of Edgartown Great Pond.
- 7:50 PM; USSS boat launches
- 7:57 PM; USSS vehicle/first responder vehicle arrives to the area of the shoreline of Edgartown Great Pond.
- 7:58 PM; First Edgartown Police vehicle arrives to the area of the shoreline.
- 7:59 PM; Second Edgartown Police vehicle arrives to the area of the shoreline.

A request has been made to obtain a copy of the above-described video and is pending its release as of the time of this report.

The state police wrote in their cover letter to Judicial Watch: "The Department conducted a diligent search of its records and is unable to locate any body worn and cruiser mounted video recordings. The Department is in the process of reviewing responsive records and will supplement this response."

How strange that Barack Obama himself was brought in for an interview regarding this apparently accidental drowning, and no mention of his involvement was made until Judicial Watch pushed for several months to receive all the relevant reports.[5]

And what did the video evidence reveal? "Why is the Secret Service hiding the video that can provide the public more information about the death of Barack Obama's personal chef?" I asked at the time. "The Secret Service's involvement in this death investigation had been treated like a state secret until Judicial Watch uncovered it."[6]

Judicial Watch sued to get access to the audio and video evidence, which was not forthcoming. But in December 2023 we did learn more details of the drowning, which were not flattering for the Secret Service. We got thirty-one pages of records that showed the identity of the companion of Obama's chef Tafari Campbell as a woman named "Ms. Taylor," who reported that "[Campbell] fell in the water and struggled for a couple of seconds before giving up and sinking underwater."

The records also showed that the Secret Service could not get the first two boats they tried to use to search for Campbell to function and had to use the groundskeeper's boat. Also, at least one, and possibly multiple, agents from the Secret Service's Little Rock, Arkansas, office were involved in the search for Campbell's body.

The records include a July 24 report from a Secret Service agent whose name is redacted that reveals the interview details—including the name—of Campbell's paddleboarding companion: "Ms. Taylor stated that Mr. Campbell was not wearing a life jacket and had no personal flotation devices aboard the paddleboard at the time of the incident."

A separate report notes how Campbell's companion "collapsed on the ground and stated that Tafari had drowned. She stated that he fell in the water and struggled for a couple of seconds before giving up and sinking underwater." The agent continued, describing how a supervisory agent and another agent "attempted to start one of the boats but had difficulties lowering the motor. I headed down with [redacted] but told her to continue down and yelled to SA [redacted] and SSA [redacted] that I would run to get the keys for our USSS boat. I sprinted to the CP [Command Post], grabbed the keys and sprinted back towards the boats. A similar issue occurred with the motor on the second boat. We jumped into a third boat belonging to the grounds-keeper and it worked without issue."

The same report notes former President Obama came to the incident scene and the search was paused so President Obama could speak to the eyewitness:

> We continued our search with flashlights. Shortly thereafter we were called to Wilson's Landing as FPOTUS Obama was there and the local Fire Department in conjunction with Massachusetts Police Department and other local agencies were setting up an Incident Command Post. He had wanted to talk with [redacted]. The first EMS/Police response we saw may have occurred within an hour. I recall seeing a small PD or Fire boat scanning the shoreline just after it was getting dark.

"It is disturbing that Secret Service boats did not work for this emergency situation," I remarked. "This new information perhaps explains why the Secret Service is still hiding video related to the tragic drowning."[7]

Indeed. The Secret Service is tasked with protecting the lives of former presidents. One would think that their boats would at least operate well enough to save someone drowning in seven feet of water. At this writing, former President Trump may be facing jail or even prison time for his conviction in the ginned-up prosecution against him, and the Secret Service is reportedly preparing to accompany him to Rikers Island, Sing Sing, or wherever the New York State Department of Corrections assigns him. One hopes his agency is better prepared than it was Martha's Vineyard.

....

Most presidents have pets around. It is believed that demonstrating affection for animals humanizes remote officials. FDR had Fala, his beloved terrier. The Kennedys had a menagerie of animals, LBJ had beagles, and Nixon (as vice president) had Checkers. Bill Clinton had Buddy the dog and Socks the cat, and the Bushes and Obamas all had dogs.

Trump, somewhat famously, had no pets. His apparent lack of interest in pets was used against him by his political opponents. In 2020, a group called Dog Lovers for Joe ran an ad showing former presidents with their dogs, pointing out that Trump didn't have a canine companion, and ending with a picture of Joe Biden nuzzling his beloved German shepherd Champ. During the campaign, Biden tweeted "Some Americans celebrate #NationalCatDay, some celebrate #NationalDogDay . . . President Trump celebrates neither. It says a lot. It's time we put a pet back in the White House."

Lots of Americans have dogs—lots—so who's to say that the dog vote didn't give Biden the margin of victory in some swing state? (Given some of our election security failures, one wonders if dogs literally do "vote"!)

But a curious event happened right after the election that made sharp observers take note that Biden's relations with our furry four-legged friends might not be as cozy as we thought.

At the end of November 2020, President-Elect Biden fractured his foot and had to wear a boot for a few weeks. Most news reports stated that Biden had been "playing" with his dog Major, but didn't get into specifics. But Biden's own account of what happened is illuminating.

"What happened," Biden explained to CNN journalist Jake Tapper, "was I got out of the shower. I got a dog and anybody who's been around my house knows—dropped, little pup dropped a ball in front of me. And for me to grab the ball.

"And I'm walking through this little alleyway to get to the bedroom," Biden continued. "And I grabbed the ball like this and he ran. And I'm joking, running after him and grab his tail. And what happened was that he slid on a throw rug. And I tripped on the rug he slid on. That's what happened. Oh man, not a very exciting story."[8]

Sorry, sir, how's that again? You were chasing the dog and pulling on his tail?

Anyone who has spent any time with dogs knows that pulling on a dog's tail is not how you play with dogs. It is painful and can cause serious injury and a biting response from the dog.

Tail pulling is also associated with aggression. The American Kennel Club recommends a picture book for children aged one through three called *Tails Are Not for Pulling* to help teach babies how to treat the family dog in order to establish good relations early on.

Basically, pulling a dog's tail is cruel and bullying. But knowing how Joe Biden treats his dogs may enlighten us to what happened next. On March 9, 2021, the White House confirmed that President Biden's dog Major "did in fact bite someone at the White House," causing a "minor injury." Press secretary Jen Psaki confirmed that the dogs "are still getting acclimated and accustomed to their new surroundings and new people."[9]

Both Major and the Bidens' older dog Champ were sent to the home of a Biden family friend on March 9, and Champ supposedly received some remedial training. On March 17, President Biden told the media, "You turn a corner, and there's two people you don't know at all. And he moves to protect. But he's a sweet dog. Eighty-five percent of the people there love him. He just—all he does is lick them and wag his tail." A week later, both dogs were sent back to the White House.[10]

Then, on March 30, 2021, the White House reported that, "President Biden's dog Major on Monday afternoon bit another employee, who then required medical attention." The encounter reportedly took place on the White House South Lawn Monday, on March 29.[11]

We've been around the block a bit over thirty years and love dogs. A dog biting strangers twice is a big deal. In fact, biting two different people can result in a judge ordering the euthanizing of a dog. Judicial Watch asked for records, received the proverbially hand to the face and so sued to get more information about Biden's dog attacks. It's not normal for a dog to keep attacking people. "The public has a right to know the details about any incident in which Secret Service personnel were injured by President Biden's dog," I said at the time. "We have no doubt that Major and Champ are good dogs, but politicians and bureaucrats can't be trusted."

It took six months, but we got the real story about Major. In August 2021 we received thirty-six pages of records from the Secret Service that showed the Bidens' dog Major was in fact responsible for numerous biting incidents of Secret Service personnel. One email notes that "at the current rate an Agent or Officer has been bitten every day this week (3/1-3/8) causing damage to attire or bruising/punctures to the skin." The documents show that agents were advised to protect their "hands/fingers" by placing their hands "in their pockets." Photos of the dog bite injuries were blacked out by the agency.

That's many more bites than Americans were told about at first.

On March 8, 2021, a Secret Service official emailed redacted Secret Service officials:

> Attached are a couple of photos from the dog bites SA [redacted] has received the [*sic*] in the last week from the First Family's pet (Major).
>
> On 3.1.21, SA [redacted] was bit by Major on [redacted] at the Lake House in Wilmington, DE. That bite caused some bruising as seen in the picture dated 3.1.21.
>
> On 3.8.21, SA [redacted] was bit by Major on [redacted] at the White House. That bite caused bruising and puncture to the skin as seen in the picture dated 3.8.21.
>
> At the current rate an Agent or Officer has been bitten every day this week (3/1-3/8) causing damage to attire or bruising/punctures to the skin.

An assistant special agent in charge forwards the message and images to Secret Service official David Cho, reporting, "Sirs, We had another dog bite incident this morning. This was the 2nd time SA [redacted] was bitten."

On March 1, 2021, a Protective Division agent notes, "This weekend in Wilmington, there were 3 minor incidents where Major nipped/brushed up and nudged Shift SAs. Panicking or running with only embolden animals so stand your ground and protect your hands/fingers by placing them in your pockets or behind your back."

The new documents show that the dogs first arrived on January 24, 2021. An email sent by a Joint Operations Center supervisor reports that:

[T]he First Families 2 dogs have arrived on the complex. Please call them out when the [sic] enter and exit the residence. Be sure and know their locations prior to opening your gates on the grounds.

   IMPACT ON COMPLEX: No impact to normal White House operations.

That same day, an agent relayed their notes from a Secret Service supervisor's meeting, writing: "Major (family pet) is not always predictable. Be careful, especially if you have to make entry during an [redacted] situation."

Two days later, on March 3, 2021, an agent details to Cho that: "Major went after the officer at [redacted]. Dr took a look. Redness on left hand. Officer back at [redacted]."

Cho asks: "Who was minding the pets? Protected or Residence/usher staff?" An agent responds: "Protectee. Usher was there as well."

On March 5, 2021, a series of emails was sent about Major attacking a White House pass holder. The Presidential Protective Division reported, "For your awareness. WHMU [White House Medical Unit] responded to the South Portico a short time ago on a UDW [Uniformed Division White House] report of a pass holder with a dog bite. The pass holder is [redacted] of the Residence Staff. He is currently being treated in the Doctor's office."

Agent David Cho, head of the Presidential Protective Division detail, asked, "Was it Major?" The other agent wrote, "Doesn't sound like it. Attempting to ascertain severity of injury. Pass holder walked out of [redacted] and dog made b-line to hm. Got his arm twice. A group was standing there at time."

An agent then responded, "Minor. Did break the skin." Quickly adding, "Sorry. Meant it was Major, the name of the younger German shepherd. He's been an issue lately." An agent adds: "Dog: Major. Injury: Minor." To which David Cho replied, "Ha! Thank you."

On March 6, 2021, Major attempted to bite again. An agent wrote:

> Major attempted to bite SA [redacted] this evening. He didn't make
> contact with agent's skin, but did bite a hole through his overcoat.
> This marks the third day in a row someone has been bitten by Major
> (Thursday USSS SA & Friday Pass Holder).
>   I just wanted you to have visibility. I think it's definitely worth
> bringing up during Monday's meeting with staff.

David Cho replied, "Copy. We passed to usher Office. FLD also passed to [redacted]. Will present to [redacted] on Monday. RTC K9 trainer [redacted] is very good at training canines. He did it for Obama, etc. we have extended that piece and will pursue again."

An agent wrote on March 8, 2021, "The dogs are being transported to Delaware and will stay there for an undetermined time. The family will use a trainer they have used previously."

Later that same day, David Cho emailed colleagues, writing, "Apparently CNN will be running a story on how a family pet bit two agents, and have now been sent to Delaware. Of course the situation is sensitive, and unsure how the information originated. Just wanted to send to you for awareness."

One colleague responded, "this is ridiculous."

Major returned to the White House in April 2021. Champ died in June 2021.

"We're sure Major is a good dog but these records show he was involved in many more biting incidents than the Biden White House has publicly acknowledged," I told the press. "It is disturbing to see a White House cover-up of numerous injuries to Secret Service and White House personnel by the Bidens' family pet."

But it turns out that Major had many more problems than we had been told. In April 2022, Judicial Watch obtained 400 pages of new records including incident reports detailing multiple attacks and damages caused to United States Secret Service (USSS) members by Major at both the White House and the Bidens' lake home in Delaware. The documents also reveal that a member of USSS who was attacked by the dog was displeased that White House Press Secretary Jen Psaki misled the press about the incident.

In an email chain dated March 9, 2021, a member of the Presidential Protective Division (PPD) expresses their anger that White House Press Secretary Jen Psaki lacked candor about the dog bite incident during a press briefing. The chain begins when a fellow agent checks on the welfare of a colleague asking, "You okay? Someone told me you got bit."

The USSS PPD agent replies, "Yes I got bit by Major on [redacted] and NO I didn't surprise the dog doing my job by being at [redacted] as the press secretary just said! Now I'm pissed. Thanks for checking in."

The initial agent replies, "SMH (shaking my head) . . . hope you didn't get hurt too bad. Take care."

A Secret Service incident report concerning a dog attack on the morning of February 28, 2021, at the Bidens' Wilmington, Delaware, lake home discloses the following:

At approximately 0900hrs, while working the AM shift for POTUS at the Wilmington, DE Lake house, SA [redacted] was walking to relieve SA [redacted] from the [redacted] location. SA [redacted] stated that [redacted] observed Major running at SA [redacted] and heard him yelling at the dog. At this point, SA [redacted] continued to walk toward SA [redacted] location and saw Major had turned in [redacted] direction running at high speed. SA [redacted] once more heard SA [redacted] yell, "Major stop!" before [redacted] turned around to avoid a direct attack. Upon turning [redacted] was

struck on [redacted] right thigh by the dog's mouth. Major
then ran across the yard towards the opposite end of the house.
SA [redacted] was shaken from this encounter, having almost
been bitten, therefore SA [redacted] held the [redacted] with
[redacted] until Major had been brought back into the residence.
SA [redacted] did not seek medical attention for this incident.

The report has a footnote regarding a photo taken a week after the
attack, showing "a bruise where Major's mouth impacted [redacted]
leg. The oval shape of injury demonstrates the outline of the dog's
closed jaws."

In an email dated June 24, 2021, regarding the February 28 incident, a Secret Service official writes: "I have taken the liberty of adding
the Uniformed Division to this email chain as I understand there have
been multiple bite/attack incidents involving Major and their officers."

A separate incident report concerning another dog attack on the
evening of February 28, 2021, at the Bidens' Wilmington, Delaware,
lake home notes:

At approximately 1900hrs, while working the PM shift for
POTUS at the Wilmington DE Lake house, SA [redacted]
was [redacted] of the residence. SA [redacted] observed
POTUS Biden walk up to the front door with the elder family
dog Champ. SA [redacted] stated that POTUS [redacted].
After several minutes of waiting, Major failed to appear and
POTUS took Champ inside closing the door behind him.
Almost immediately after the door had shut, SA [redacted]
observed Major running at [redacted] full stride from the main
driveway. SA [redacted] quickly made an effort to seek shelter
inside [redacted]. Despite the attempt, Major intercepted
SA [redacted] and bit down on [redacted] left forearm. SA

[redacted] quickly shook Major off of [redacted] arm and once more attempted to [redacted] to avoid further attack. In so doing, SA [redacted] briefly turned [redacted] back on Major and the dog bit [redacted] a second time on the right buttock. Fortunately, despite the two injuries, SA [redacted] was able to [redacted], separating [redacted] self from the animal. Approximately 15 minutes after this attack, POTUS Biden opened the front door to let Major into the residence. At this point, SA [redacted] stated the dog then went inside and POTUS [redacted]. SA [redacted], shaken by the ordeal, took a relief push to inspect [redacted] injury at the [redacted]. He then [redacted] and finished the remainder of [redacted] shift despite the discomfort.

A footnote points out: "NOTE—The attack on SA [redacted] occurred less than 12 hours after the first attack on SA [redacted]."

An incident report stemming from a March 6, 2021, dog attack discloses the following:

As the dog came around the corner from the diplomatic room [of the White House], he [Major] locked eyes with SA [redacted]. SA [redacted] having been a [redacted] his entire life, knew from this moment of eye contact with Major that something serious was about to go down. Major advanced on SA [redacted] and quickened pace in the final 10ft of distance. The dog then attempted to bite SA [redacted] left arm but was only able to lock teeth on his overcoat as he stepped aside from the attack. The First Lady [redacted]; however the coat was torn during the altercation. The President witnessed the First Lady [redacted] and [redacted] before moving the entire party onto the residence elevator.

A photo is attached to the email, and a footnote in the email reads: "The image attached was taken approximately one month after the attack and shows the severity of the bite through SA [redacted] wool overcoat. (The overcoat is valued at >$500. As of this date, SA [redacted] has not been compensated for the damage.)"

A Secret Service incident report concerning a dog attack on the morning of March 8, 2021, at the White House discloses the following:

> At approximately 0700hrs, while working the AM shift for POTUS at the White House, SA [redacted] was positioned at the 2nd Floor [redacted] in the residence. Around this same time, the First Lady [redacted] to the 2nd floor residence. Without warning or provocation, Major barked loudly at SA [redacted] and charged at [redacted]. Having no time to seek cover from the attack, SA [redacted] turned away from the dog as he bit into [redacted] right leg. The First Lady [redacted]. The First Lady then [redacted] into the residence elevator and down to the ground floor [redacted]. ATSAIC [assistant to the special agent-in-charge] [redacted]. [Redacted] immediate supervisor, heard the barking from the ground floor and immediately came to the 2nd floor post to check on SA [redacted] status. He instructed [redacted] to take a picture of the injury and seek medical evaluation from the White House doctor on the ground floor. At approximately 0800, the White House nurse on duty [redacted]. Despite all this, [redacted] managed to complete the remainder of [redacted] shift even with [redacted] on [redacted] right leg.

A footnote indicates that photos, which were redacted, are attached, and states: "SA [redacted] injury cannot be described in any other term than 'severe.' [Redacted] is the only known PPD agent to have suffered two attacks from Major in less than 10 days. (As of this date, [redacted] has received no compensation for either injury.)"

A Secret Service email concerning a dog attack on the morning of May 12, 2021, at the White House discloses the following:

> On May 12th, 2021 around 630-645am. The First Lady brought Major down to take him outside before movement to an in town site. The First Lady and the Usher were standing next to me at [redacted] along with a [redacted]. I was standing back against the wall as to leave space for the First Lady and Major who was on a leash. Out of nowhere the dog jumps and bites the sleeve of my suit jacket missing my arm (front teeth just scratching the top of the skin). As I lift my arm up the dog was still attached to my suit jacket and the First Lady was attempting to pull the dog off of me via the leash. Once the dog let go, the First Lady ran into the Dip[lomatic Reception] room with the dog. The usher came out to see how I was. Later [redacted] said the First Lady [redacted]. SAIC Cho was at my post 20 min later to check on my well-being.

In a memo prepared by Secret Service management regarding a May 13, 2021, meeting several managers had with the Secret Service agent who was attacked by Major on March 6, one of the officials "explained the delicateness of the situation, in terms of potential damage in the trust of our protectees."

In a May 11, 2021, email, a Secret Service agent describes the dog bite incident and is criticized for adding the additional details:

> I have attached yet another revision to the SSF3361. In hindsight, I agree that the brief description of the nature of the dog bite damage to my wool overcoat was lacking in sufficient details.

I included the following as well as the language you felt at liberty to provide:

"On the evening of March 6th 2021 I was working an evening shift at the White House as per my usual duties. While leading the President and First Lady back from the Tennis pavilion to the Residence, Major, the younger of the First Family's two dogs, was [redacted] the First Lady in the Diplomatic Reception Room. As Major came around the corner, he attacked me unprovoked, tearing the wool overcoat I was wearing that evening. This attack occurred through no fault of my own and I could not avoid this unusual circumstance due to the nature and requirements of my position."

After providing the additional details, the agent is admonished for providing too much detail, with another official telling him, "Please submit with the language that has been approved by LEG [legal office]. Unless you dispute anything in the verbiage that was presented to you, there shouldn't be a need to embellish with additional details that aren't required for approval."

That official's email is forwarded with criticism of the additional detail, "SA [redacted] verbiage was deemed excessively detailed and inappropriate. I was asked to have him submit with the language that has already been approved by LEG [legal office]. Not sure if he will or not. I don't think it's about the money anymore."

In a March 1, 2021, Secret Service "PPD [Presidential Protective Division] Supervisors Meeting Notes" memo, one bullet entry under the heading "SAIC CHO" [then-Special Agent-in-Charge David Cho] reads "First Family Pet Behavior."

In a March 5, 2021, email, a redacted Secret Service official advises White House officials:

For your awareness, WHMU [White House Medical Unit] responded to the South Portico a short time ago on a UDW [Uniformed Division White House] report of a pass holder with a dog bite.

In an email dated March 9, 2021, with the subject line "Supervisor's Meeting Notes," a redacted Secret Service official advises other agents about the press coverage:

Family pets are both in Wilmington. Younger pet bit a Shift SA [special agent] yesterday. Staff/first family are getting him a full time trainer to correct his behavior in Wilmington. . . . The biting incident is in the news now (Google it). Just another reminder that the press is always looking for a story. Maintain awareness of your conversations and social media presence. We do not want and cannot have a press lead attributed to us.

In an email dated March 16, 2021, an assistant to the special agent-in-charge writes to a supervisory program manager in the Presidential Protective Division regarding a reimbursement request for a torn special agent's overcoat, noting: "This is reimbursement of an article of clothing that was damaged by a family pet. Sending this to you direct to limit distribution."

The recipient replies, "Thank you Sir. To limit distribution, I will handle this directly with [redacted] in Budget for reimbursement."[12]

"These documents show Major was a dangerous dog and the Biden White House lied about it, placing Secret Service and other White House personnel at needless risk," I said. "And it seems the Secret Service management seemed more concerned about managing press relations than taking care of its agents. In fact, the agency is still withholding information about this mess!"[13]

In December 2021, the Bidens announced that they had been given a new, three-week old German shepherd puppy for Christmas by James Biden, the president's brother, and the new dog, named Commander, would take up permanent residence at the White House. Major, regretfully, would retire to the home of a family friend in Delaware. Commander, as a puppy, would presumably receive the early good training that Major, a shelter dog, may have never received.

But within a year or so of Commander taking over as First Dog, we were alerted behind the scenes that he was demonstrating aggressive behavior. So in April 2023 Judicial Watch filed a suit asking for records regarding Commander. The information we received over the next year was deeply shocking. According to official Secret Service records, Commander had been involved in at least twenty-three biting incidents, some of them quite serious. What follows is an abbreviated summary of the attacks, because the detail is overwhelming.

On November 3, 2022, a Secret Service official at "JOCATDESK" [Joint Operations Center Assistant to the Special Agent in Charge] emailed colleagues in the Presidential Protective Division:

> Commander bite [*sic*] UD [Uniform Division] officer [redacted] at post [redacted] two times, one time in the upper right arm and a second bite on the officer's thigh. WH [White House] medical treated the officer and made the decision to have [redacted] transported to [redacted] Hospital.

An email later that day from a captain of the Uniform Division, whose name is redacted, states that he was advised that the dog was up-to-date on all vaccines.

A November 4, 2022, an email report added details regarding the previous day's attack. A Division officer, after being bitten in the arm and thigh, had to use a steel cart to shield himself from another attack.

In a November 5, 2022, an email exchange between a Uniformed Division officer and the November 3 attack victim, the first officer asks, "Doing alright [redacted]? That's freaking crazy that stupid dog—rolling my eyes [redacted]." The victim replies, "My leg and arm still hurts. He bit me twice and ran at me twice." The colleague replies, "What a joke [redacted]—if it wasn't their dog he would already have been put down—freaking clown needs a muzzle—hope you get to feeling better [redacted]."

In an email dated October 26, 2022, a Uniformed Division officer reports to colleagues:

> Commander has been exhibiting extremely aggressive behavior. Today, while posted, he came charging at me. The First Lady couldn't regain control of commander [sic] and he continued to circle me. I believe it's only a matter of time before an agent/officer is attacked or bit.
>
> He would have bit me today if I didn't step towards him a couple different times. It was bad enough that the agent on the detail asked if I got bit—just so you're aware.

A November 10, 2022, Secret Service memorandum describes an incident that occurred with Commander earlier in the day. While patrolling the White House grounds, a Uniformed Division Secret Service officer was attacked by Commander while First Lady Jill Biden was walking him in the Kennedy Garden. The officer was bitten on the left thigh, and subsequently experienced "bruising, tenderness and pain in the bite area." He was tended to by the White House medical unit and filed a workplace injury report with OSHA [Occupational Safety and Health Administration].

On December 11, 2022, a USSS Special Agent in the Presidential Protective Division was attacked in the evening on the South Grounds by Commander after President Biden let the dog off the leash outside the White House. He writes:

> The injuries included a bite to the left forearm resulting in bruising and approximately a 1 ½ cm cut and a bite to the right hand on the thumb resulting a 1 cm cut. I received treatment from White House Medical from LTC [redacted]. The injuries were [redacted] and I returned to work the rest of my shift.

In a heavily redacted December 24, 2022, email exchange with the subject line "Matters of extreme concern," a Secret Service Inspector reports to colleagues on the December 23 incident:

> I attended officials roll call [redacted] this afternoon. The dog bite issue came up again today. Please see the attached email chain written last evening. Apparently, Officer [redacted] was bitten while posted at [redacted] yesterday. Nearly every official in the room with me today spoke about specific incidents surrounding the First Family's dog.

The remainder of the email, and a response to it, is redacted. The inspector's email is then forwarded by an official to Uniformed Division Chief Alfonso Dyson by one of the recipients, who writes, "FYSA [for your situational awareness] . . . PPD [Presidential Protection Division] is being notified of the latest incident, but we need to address this issue ASAP collectively."

A January 2, 2023, email chain describes an incident with Commander involving a Technical Security Investigator who was looking into an alarm going off at the Bidens' Wilmington lake house. He was attacked by the dog when the house sitter opened the front door to talk to the agent.

On June 15, 2023, Dep. Asst. Dir. Darryl Volpicelli was sent a report via email regarding an agent who received a "deep bite" by Commander while "inside the Kennedy Garden." The incident shut down East Wing tours for twenty minutes.

A January 28, 2023, email chain discusses three biting incidents, "two incidents today and one yesterday." Later that day, a Presidential Protection Division official whose name is redacted emails Senior White House Advisor Anthony Bernal that "Commander bit one of the Navy Staff" who worked at Camp David.

On July 29, 2023, nearly six weeks after agents had compiled a list of twenty-two bite incidents, another attack of an agent occurred at the Bidens' beach house. The July 30 incident report indicates:

> Commander ran towards the direction of post [redacted] booth and bit SA [redacted] in the left forearm. Causing a severe, deep open wound. As a result of the attack SA [redacted] started to loose [*sic*] a significant amount of blood from [redacted] arm. SA [redacted] remained calm and walked away from the area looking for help.[14]

Finally, in October 2023 Commander was removed and sent to Delaware permanently. A source has informed Judicial Watch that President Biden mistreats his dogs, punching and kicking them. Given the dog attacks, Biden should thankful no one was injured or killed. Instead, as the *New York Times* reports, "When the first biting incident involving Major was reported, Mr. Biden told a friend that 'it didn't happen' and that someone was lying"! Could it be any clearer that Biden has contempt for the Secret Service personnel protecting him?

These Biden dog attack documents raise fundamental questions about President Biden and the Secret Service. This is a special sort of craziness and corruption where a president and first lady would allow their dog to repeatedly attack two dozen Secret Service and White House personnel, and keep it hidden.

But more than that, the behavior of President Biden's dogs tells us something frightening about Joe Biden the man. It reveals the cruelty and arrogance of a man who behaves as a bully. Who is infamous for making nasty, cutting remarks toward his subordinates. Who smiles sickly when his political opponent is found guilty in a sham trial.

I've often made the observation that "abusers" in elected and other powerful position are responsible for the attacks on our constitutional rights, outrageous corruption and other misconduct.

Is Biden not the Abuser-in-Chief in obliviously allowing his dog to attack government employees—including the Secret Service personnel who are willing to risk their lives to protect him and his family?

If he risks the safety and lives of Secret Service personnel, why would we be surprised that we see other serious abuses that affect the whole country emanating from his White House?

CONCLUSION

Our nation confronts extraordinarily serious challenges. Four years ago, in my last book, *A Republic Under Assault: the Left's Ongoing Attack on American Freedom*, I wrote

> Unfortunately, one critical expression and truism has become much more of a cliché than a call to arms over the last few decades. The Left has seen to that.
> That truism: "Freedom isn't free."
> Fewer and fewer people ever think about that saying, and only people like us know it to be true.
> Obama and Clinton operatives, the Deep State, and their allies were counting on that new and sad reality to help them "take down" President Trump. They failed, but have not given up.

That was a serious warning, but it wasn't strong enough.

I'm not sure we could have predicted how bad things would get. The Left subverted political and social norms by misusing a public health crisis, applauding mob violence and arson that caused billions of dollars of damage, and then rammed untested and irregular balloting and vote counting procedures through the courts.

Using a compromised and weakened man in the White House, the Left immediately erased our borders, inviting in untold millions of un-vetted migrants. Even while children sat in front of screens instead of at school desks because of the alleged danger of infection, Third World itinerants were showing up in major metros with polio, tuberculosis, and Chagas disease.

Even at Ellis Island, where millions of Americans' forebears passed through on their way into the American midstream, a sizeable percent-age of would-be immigrants were sent back home after failing medi-cal and psychological exams. Or they were referred for treatment. But their names were recorded, and we had a sense of who they were.

No civilized nation permits an unchecked flow of human move-ment to enter its borders with no regard for their past or their future intentions.

But we do.

The present crisis often brings to my mind the title of James Burn-ham's famous book *Suicide of the West*. How is the border invasion, the embrace of political rioting and jailing, the contempt the Consti-tution and our nation's founding anything other than the potential suicidal ideations of a declining political culture. Burnham writing in the 1960s was direct in his diagnosis:

> For the past two generations Western civilization has been shrinking; the amount of territory, and the number of persons relative to the world population, that the West rules have much and rapidly declined.
>
> A generation or two later, can we say the diagnosis has improved for us?

The Left and its deep state minions are going all out to accelerate our national (and civilizational) decline. Were they concerned about the radical anarchists who attacked cops and burned downtowns through the summer of 2020? Did they fret about the foreign terrorist cells that federal law enforcement were warning are already in place? No.

The real problem, we were told, was parents who showed up at school board meetings, wanting to know why their small children were being encouraged to consider getting sex change operations, or being told that their complexion morally implicated them in the trans-Atlantic slave trade.

The problem, we were told, is Catholics who want to attend traditional Latin Mass. And according to Harvard, the problem is parents who homeschool.

The problem, if we get down to it, is *us*. You and I, and another 150 million or so Americans who want to live normal lives, mind our own business, raise our kids in safe communities, worship as we wish, and hopefully save a few bucks, are a fly in the witches' ointment of Marxist "equity" that the Left wants to impose upon every square inch of the United States of America.

That's where you come in. Because your life, with whatever success you have attained through grit, wit, and spit is an embarrassment to the regime. It mocks their wicked ideals and shows how the enduring American values of regulated liberty and republican self-government still work, if they are allowed to.

The Leftist agenda works nowhere, so it must be imposed everywhere.

Ronald Reagan, speaking in 1975, observed, "Socialists ignore the side of man that is the spirit. They can provide you shelter, fill your belly with bacon and beans, treat you when you're ill, all the things guaranteed to a prisoner or a slave. They don't understand that we also dream."

I would actually quibble with President Reagan here. Socialists may *promise* to fill your belly and treat you when you're ill, but they invariably fail. They can't even do the basics.

But Reagan was absolutely correct in his larger point, which is that socialists have no sense of human attainment besides using people as cogs to produce more socialism. They really do see humanity as slaves, bound for life to serve the master of Progress.

The Left Borg wants us to think that resistance is futile to their dangerous, anti-American agenda. But you know better. Fighting for America is never futile. It is our duty to stand strong—for our children and the generations to come. It is the American way!

I know it seems like things are dire. And I won't beat around the bush, they are. Our president is compromised by his family's foreign racketeering. This corruption has weakened America and made us less safe.

In addition to the corruption crisis, we're in a revolutionary period where the communists think they can undo our republican form of government.

All I can say is: thank Heaven for Judicial Watch.

Judicial Watch is America's largest and most effective government watchdog group. The Left starts sweating when we start FOIAing.

The rule of battered but still stands—as powerfully demonstrated by Judicial Watch's success in the courts for transparency, cleaner elections and against the work racist agenda.

I am so proud to be part of Judicial Watch, because we have absorbed the basic meaning of our Founding documents—that all men are created equal—and taken it upon ourselves to vindicate for the core rights of citizens against the deceit and machinations of the government which is supposed to serve them. As darkness threatens our nation, Judicial Watch will continue to cast its light into dank corners where the Deep State hides its secrets, and we will continue to insist that NO MAN IS ABOVE THE LAW.

I will close with heartening remarks I made to a national audience earlier this year:

Get up, stand up for freedom! Stand up against the Extremist Left! Stand up for our borders and sovereignty! Stand up against corruption! Stand up for transparency! Stand up for our children! Stand up for Life! Stand up for the Rule of Law! Stand up for Free Speech and your other God-given rights! Stand up for the Constitution and the American revolution for liberty it represents!

We have no choice but to win. You all must be heroes for the republic!

God bless you and God bless America.

ACKNOWLEDGMENTS

This book and all that went into it represents the collaborative efforts of the Judicial Watch team, whose patriotism, work ethic, and vision have built Judicial Watch into one of the most significant civic organizations in the history of our country. My fellow board members: Paul Orfanedes, our Director of Litigation, and Chris Farrell, our Director of Research and Investigations, have helped me lead our team in mounting continual successes in pursuit of the rule of law. And in further testament to the voluntary spirit of the great American nation, none of our achievement would have been possible without the generous backing of millions of Americans who are Judicial Watch supporters and members.

Of course, the families of our staff deserve a special note of thanks, as their steadfast support is also essential to our success. And for those of you who helped me directly in writing *Rights and Freedoms in Peril*, thank you for ensuring the success of this essential educational effort. I am very grateful to the talented and dedicated team at Simon & Schuster, Threshold Editions, who have now worked with me—God bless them—on four books.

My editor, Paul Choix, operates with consummate professionalism, and his guidance, direction, and suggestions have been invaluable.

ACKNOWLEDGMENTS

Executive editor Natasha Simons has been a longtime champion of getting the Judicial Watch message to the people, and her persistent advocacy of this project has been indispensable. Our publisher, Jennifer Bergstrom, and associate publisher, Jennifer Long, deserve the eternal gratitude of Judicial Watch. We are honored to have entrusted our important content to you, and we're grateful for the team you have gathered to tend to the details of making and marketing this book. We truly value the efforts of publicist Jill Siegel and associate marketing director Kell Wilson in helping to spread the word about this title. Thank you for working closely with our team to ensure the best coverage possible for our book. A special thanks is due to managing editor Caroline Pallotta; designer Davina Mock; and art director Lisa Litwack and deputy art director John Vairo for investing their talents to fashion and produce a book whose visual and physical attributes are befitting the important content it conveys. Seth Barron provided valuable insights on style and content. And special thanks to Frank Breeden, our literary agent, who has shepherded us patiently through the years in our publishing endeavors!

NOTES

CHAPTER 1: PLANNED CHAOS AT THE BORDER

1. White House, "Fact Sheet: President-Elect Biden's Day One Executive Actions Deliver Relief for Families Across America amid Converging Crises," January 20, 2021, https://www.whitehouse .gov/briefing-room/statements-releases/2021/01/20/fact-sheet -president-elect-bidens-day-one-executive-actions-deliver-re lief-for-families-across-america-amid-converging-crises/.

2. "Town Hall with Frm Vice President Joe Biden, Presidential Candidate," moderated by Anderson Cooper, CNN, February 20, 2020, https://transcripts.cnn.com/show/se /date/2020-02-20/segment/03.

3. Nidhi Prakash, "Joe Biden's Campaign Reversed and Said He's Supporting a Moratorium on Deportations," Buzzfeed News, February 22, 2020, https://www.buzzfeednews.com/article /nidhiprakash/joe-biden-nevada-caucus-2020-deportations.

4. Nick Miroff, " 'Kids in Cages': It's True That Obama Built the Cages at the Border. But Trump's 'Zero Tolerance' Immigration Policy Had No Precedent," *Washington Post*, October 23, 2020,

https://www.washingtonpost.com/immigration/kids-in-cages
-debate-trump-obama/2020/10/23/8ff96f3c-1532-11eb-82af
-864652063d61_story.html.

5. Judicial Watch press release, March 23, 2021.

6. FAIR newsletter, May 2021.

7. "Southwest Land Border Encounters," U.S. Customs and Border
Protection, July 15, 2024, https://www.cbp.gov/newsroom/stats
/southwest-land-border-encounters.

8. Judicial Watch press release, May 6, 2021.

9. Judicial Watch press release, August 4, 2021.

10. Judicial Watch press release, December 22, 2022.

11. Judicial Watch press release, February 9, 2022.

12. Ibid.

13. Todd Bensman, "Government Admission: Biden Parole Flights
Create Security 'Vulnerabilities' at U.S. Airports," Center for
Immigration Studies, March 4, 2024, https://cis.org/Bensman
/Government-Admission-Biden-Parole-Flights-Create-Security
-Vulnerabilities-US-Airports.

14. "Operation Lone Star," Office of the Texas Governor, https://
gov.texas.gov/operationlonestar.

15. John Gramlich, "Migrant Encounters at the U.S.-Mexico Border
Hit a Record High at the End of 2023," Pew Research Center,
February 15, 2024, https://www.pewresearch.org/short-reads
/2024/02/15/migrant-encounters-at-the-us-mexico-border-hit
-a-record-high-at-the-end-of-2023/.

16. Mohammad Fazel Zarandi, Jonathan S. Feinstein, and Edward H. Kaplan, "Yale Study Finds Twice as Many Undocumented Immigrants as Previous Estimates," Yale Insights, September 21, 2018, https://insights.som.yale.edu/insights/yale-study-finds-twice-as -many-undocumented-immigrants-as-previous-estimates.

17. Judicial Watch press release, March 19, 2024.

18. MaryAnn Martinez, "Border Patrol Admits It's Responsible for Open Floodgates in Arizona Border Wall," *New York Post*, August 22, 2023, https://nypost.com/2023/08/22/border-patrol -admits-its-responsible-for-open-floodgates-in-arizona-border-wall/.

19. Judicial Watch press release, March 20, 2023.

20. Judicial Watch press release, April 30, 2020.

21. Seth Barron, "Cash for Illegal Aliens," *City Journal*, April 12, 2021, https://www.city-journal.org/article/cash-for-illegal-aliens.

22. Greg Abbott (@GregAbbott_TX), "Congresswoman from New York explains why she supports illegal immigration: 'I need more people in my district JUST FOR REDISTRICTING PURPOSES.' These Democrats are looking out for themselves, not for America," X, January 9, 2024, https://x.com/GregAbbott_TX/status /1744897632651116550?lang=en.

CHAPTER 2: LAWFARE TARGETING TRUMP

1. Alexander Soros (@AlexanderSoros), X, May 31, 2024, https://x .com/AlexanderSoros/status/1796614879656267871.

2. Judicial Watch press release, July 7, 2023.

3. Glenn Kessler, Salvador Rizzo, and Meg Kelly, "Trump's Falseor

Misleading Claims Total 30,572 over 4 Years," *Washington Post,* January 24, 2021, https://www.washingtonpost.com/politics /2021/01/24/trumps-false-or-misleading-claims-total-30573 -over-four-years/.

4. Judicial Watch press release, March 13, 2024.

5. United States of America v. Donald J. Trump, case 1:23-cr-00257-TSC, document 1, filed August 1, 2023, https://www .justice.gov/storage/US_v_Trump_23_cr_257.pdf.

6. United States of America v. Donald J. Trump, Waltine Nauta, and Carlos De Oliveira, Case 9:23-cr-80101-AMC, document 85, filed July 7, 2023, https://www.justice.gov/storage/US-v -Trump-Nauta-De-Oliveira-23-80101.pdf.

7. Michael Bekesha, "Trump's Boxes and Clinton's Sock Drawer," *Wall Street Journal,* June 13, 2023, https://www .wsj.com/articles/clintons-sock-drawer-and-trumps-indict ment-documents-pra-personal-files-13986b28?mod=article _inline.

8. Tom Fitton (@TomFitton), X, February 26, 2024, https://x .com/TomFitton/status/1762140027511857280.

9. Emma-Jo Morris and Gabrielle Fonrouge, "Smoking-Gun Email Reveals How Hunter Biden Introduced Ukrainian Businessman to VP Dad," *New York Post,* October 14, 2020, https://nypost .com/2020/10/14/email-reveals-how-hunter-biden-introduced -ukrainian-biz-man-to-dad/.

10. Matt Taibbi (@mtaibbi), X, December 2, 2022, https://x.com /mtaibbi/status/1598827602403160064?s=20&t=qYoM28 sooi27kWaEU7mAJw.

CHAPTER 3: DIVERSITY SCAMS AND PARTY SPOILS

1. Kamala Harris, "There's a big difference between equality and equity," Facebook, November 1, 2020, https://www.facebook.com/watch/?v=1731574083660306.

2. White House, "Fact Sheet: President-Elect Biden's Day One Executive Actions Deliver Relief for Families Across America amid Converging Crises," January 20, 2021, https://www.whitehouse.gov/briefing-room/statements-releases/2021/01/20/fact-sheet-president-elect-bidens-day-one-executive-actions-deliver-relief-for-families-across-america-amid-converging-crises/.

3. Secretary of Defense Lloyd Austin, "Memorandum for Senior Pentagon Leadership," February 5, 2021, https://media.defense.gov/2021/Feb/05/2002577485/-1/-1/0/STAND-DOWN-TO-ADDRESS-EXTREMISM-IN-THE-RANKS.PDF.

4. Lieutenant Colonel Tommy Waller, "Extremism on Duty," American Mind, February 28, 2024, https://americanmind.org/salvo/extremism-on-duty/.

5. Bishop Garrison (@BishopGarrison), X, July 27, 2019, https://x.com/BishopGarrison/status/1155283103025369094.

6. "History," Defense Equal Opportunity Management Institute, https://www.defenseculture.mil/About-DEOMI/History/.

7. Judicial Watch press release, July 16, 2020.

8. "JW v DOD Air Force Academy CRT Records 03510 pgs 115–141," Judicial Watch, July 6, 2023, https://www.judicial

watch.org/documents/jw-v-dod-air-force-academy-crt-records
-03510-pgs-115-141/.

9. "JW v DOD Air Force Academy CRT Records 03510
pgs 450–453," Judicial Watch, July 6, 2023, https://www
.judicialwatch.org/documents/jw-v-dod-air-force-academy
-crt-records-03510-pgs-450-453/.

10. "MCPS Anti-Racism Tags," Judicial Watch, https://www.judi
cialwatch.org/documents/tags/mcps-anti-racism/.

11. Judicial Watch press release, May 19, 2021.

12. Judicial Watch press release, October 8, 2021.

13. Judicial Watch press release, March 8, 2024.

14. "Crest v Padilla complaint 37513 pg 3," Judicial Watch,
October 2, 2020, https://www.judicialwatch.org/documents
/crest-v-padilla-complaint-37513-pg-3/.

15. Judicial Watch press release, November 30, 2021.

16. "Crest v Padilla Verdict CA May 2022 27561, Judicial Watch,
May 16, 2022, https://www.judicialwatch.org/documents
/crest-v-padilla-verdict-ca-may-2022/.

17. Judicial Watch press release, January 29, 2024.

18. Judicial Watch press release, May 23, 2024.

CHAPTER 4: THE COVID COVERUP

1. "JW v HHS Wuhan August 31 2021 00696," Judicial Watch,
October 18, 2021, https://www.judicialwatch.org/documents
/jw-v-hhs-wuhan-august-31-2021-00696/.

2. "JW v HHS Wuhan August 31 2021 00696 pgs 12–18," Judicial Watch, December 7, 2021, https://www.judicialwatch.org /documents/jw-v-hhs-wuhan-august-31-2021-00696-pgs -12-18/.

3. Judicial Watch press release, December 7, 2021.

4. Judicial Watch press release, November 10, 2022.

5. Judicial Watch press release, December 7, 2021.

CHAPTER 5: AN ELECTION UNLIKE ANY OTHER

1. Office of the Director of National Intelligence, *Assessing Russian Activities and intentions in Recent US Elections,* January 6, 2017, https://www.intelligence.senate.gov/sites/default/files/docu ments/ICA_2017_01.pdf.

2. Cyber and Infrastructure Security Agency, "Joint Statement from Elections Infrastructure Government Coordinating Council and the Election Infrastructure Sector Coordinating Executive Committees," November 12, 2020, https://www.cisa.gov/news-events /news/joint-statement-elections-infrastructure-government-coor dinating-council-election.

3. "The National Voter Registration Act of 1993," Civil Rights Division, U.S. Department of Justice, July 20, 2020, https://www .justice.gov/crt/national-voter-registration-act-1993-nvra.

4. Judicial Watch press release, January 2, 2020.

5. Judicial Watch press release, April 9, 2020.

6. "Under Threat of Lawsuit, Allegheny Co. Purging 69,000 Inactive Voters from Rolls," CBS News, January 14, 2020,

https://www.cbsnews.com/pittsburgh/news/allegheny-county
-board-of-elections-voter-rolls/.

7. RJ Reinhart, "Faith in Elections in Relatively Short Supply in
   U.S.," Gallup News, February 13, 2020, https://news
   .gallup.com/poll/285608/faith-elections-relatively-short
   -supply.aspx.

8. The Editorial Board, "More Vindication for Voter ID,"
   Wall Street Journal, February 7, 2023, https://www.wsj.com
   /articles/voter-id-laws-pnas-study-democrats-republicans-joe
   -biden-11675811901.

9. Commission on Federal Election Reform, *Building Confidence
   in U.S. Elections,* Center for Democracy and Election Management, American University, September 2005, https://www
   .eac.gov/sites/default/files/eac_assets/1/6/Exhibit%20M
   .PDF.

10. "One in Eight Voter Registrations Inaccurate; 51 Million
    Citizens Unregistered," press release, Pew Charitable Trusts, Feb-
    ruary 14, 2012, https://www.pewtrusts.org/en/about/news
    -room/press-releases-and-statements/2012/02/14/pew-one
    -in-eight-voter-registrations-inaccurate-51-million-citizens-un
    registered.

11. Judicial Watch press release, January 23, 2023.

12. Rodney Davis, *Report: Political Weaponization of Ballot
    Harvesting in California*, United States House of Represen-
    tatives Committee on house Administration, May 13, 2020,
    https://republicans-cha.house.gov/_cache/files/5/3/53579689
    -94e4-4479-8a8a-f37eecf11baf/05130FED2B29AF93C

0F7E7E85C9ABFA8.ca-ballot-harvesting-report-final
-0.pdf.

13. Judicial Watch press release, April 27, 2021.

14. Judicial Watch press release, May 25, 2022.

CHAPTER 6: THE BIG LIE

1. Lisa Desjardins and Meredith Lee, "Electrocuted, Beaten, Abused:
Capitol Police Recall Their Own 'Vulnerability' on Jan. 6,"
PBS News, July 27, 2021, https://www.pbs.org/newshour
/show/electrocuted-beaten-abused-capitol-police-recall-their
-own-vulnerability-on-jan-6.

2. "00401 Tags," Judicial Watch, https://www.judicialwatch.org
/documents/tags/00401/.

3. Ryan Nobles and Zachary Cohen, "Jim Jordan Sent One of the
Texts Revealed by January 6 Committee," CNN, December 16,
2021, https://www.cnn.com/2021/12/15/politics/jim-jordan
-mark-meadows-text/index.html.

4. Emily Jacobs, "AOC Blasted for Exaggerating Her 'Trauma'
from Capitol Riot Experience," *New York Post,* February 4,
2021, https://nypost.com/2021/02/04/aoc-blasted-for-exagger
ating-capitol-riot-experience/.

5. Judicial Watch press release, October 12, 2023.

6. Jim Banks et al., *Report of Investigation: Security Failures at the
United States Capitol on January 6, 2021,* December 21, 2022,
https://banks.house.gov/uploadedfiles/final_report_of_investiga
tion_real.pdf.

7. Judicial Watch press release, January 5, 2024.

8. Judicial Watch press release, January 6, 2023.

CHAPTER 7: BALLOONS, DOGS, AND A MYSTERIOUS DISAPPEARANCE

1. Judicial Watch press release, August 6, 2021.

2. "02111 Tags," Judicial Watch, https://www.judicialwatch.org/documents/tags/02111/.

3. Judicial Watch press release, January 25, 2022.

4. "Edgartown PD Obama Chef Tafari Campbell PRL August 2023 pgs 5–16," Judicial Watch, August 24, 2023, https://www.judicialwatch.org/documents/edgartown-pd-obama-chef-tafari-campbell-prl-august-2023-pgs-5-16/.

5. "Mass State Police Obama Chef Tafari Campbell October 2023," Judicial Watch, October 19, 2023, https://www.judicialwatch.org/documents/mass-state-police-obama-chef-tafari-campbell-october-2023/.

6. Judicial Watch press release, October 27, 2023.

7. Judicial Watch press release, December 12, 2023.

8. "Interview with President-Elect Joe Biden and Vice President–Elect Kamala Harris," interview by Jake Tapper, CNN, December 3, 2020, https://transcripts.cnn.com/show/se/date/2020-12-03/segment/01.

9. Kate Bennett, "Biden's German Shepherd Has Aggressive Incident and Is Sent Back to Delaware," CNN, March 10, 2021, https://www.cnn.com/2021/03/08/politics/president-joe-biden-white-house-dogs/index.html.

10. Brian Naylor, "Biden Defends Major as 'a Sweet Dog' Just in Need of Some Training," March 17, 2021, https://www.npr .org/2021/03/17/978116575/biden-defends-major-as-a-sweet -dog-just-in-need-of-some-training.

11. Kate Bennett, "Bidens' Dog Major Involved in Another Biting Incident," CNN, March 31, 2021, https://www.cnn.com /2021/03/30/politics/major-biden-dog-white-house/index.html.

12. "01194 Tags," Judicial Watch, https://www.judicialwatch.org /documents/tags/01194/.

13. Judicial Watch press release, April 13, 2022.

14. "JW v DHS Biden Dog 02960 Pg 265," Judicial Watch, February 27, 2024, https://www.judicialwatch.org/documents/jw-v -dhs-biden-dog-02960-pg-265/.